ideals

Christmas
COOKBOOK

Chestnuts roasting by the fireside . . . cookies baking in the oven, desserts being decorated . . . a blending of traditional and heirloom family favorites with new recipes being tried for the first time to become, perhaps, the heirloom family recipes of the future.

It's Christmas!

And in the IDEALS CHRISTMAS COOKBOOK we've gathered together recipes that have been tested through the years, as well as some brand-new ones . . . from appetizers to beverages to candies and desserts . . . casseroles to meats and poultry . . . gifts which you will want to make and bake in your kitchen to share with family and friends . . . as well as some very special menus for your Christmas dinner and New Year's Eve buffet.

Generously sprinkled throughout the entire cookbook are bits and pieces of poetry . . . a touch of photography . . . to make this special IDEALS CHRISTMAS COOKBOOK a keepsake for you, and for you to share with your very special friends . . .

. . . not just before and during the Christmas season, but throughout the year.

IDEALS PUBLISHING CORP., MILWAUKEE, WIS. 53201
© COPYRIGHT MCMLXXV, PRINTED AND BOUND IN U.S.A.

Seventh Printing

CONTENTS

APPETIZERS	3	CAKES	28
BEVERAGES	6	TORTES	32
SOUPS	8	PIES	34
SALADS	9	PUDDINGS	38
VEGETABLES	13	DESSERTS	40
CASSEROLES	16	COOKIES	47
MEATS	18	CANDIES	52
POULTRY	22	NEW YEAR'S EVE BUFFET	56
BREADS	25	GIFTS FROM THE KITCHEN	59

CHRISTMAS DINNER 63

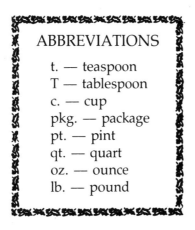

ABBREVIATIONS

t. — teaspoon
T — tablespoon
c. — cup
pkg. — package
pt. — pint
qt. — quart
oz. — ounce
lb. — pound

Photo Credits

American Meat Institute: p. 21 (bottom); Campbell Soup Co.: pp. 8, 56-57; General Foods: pp. 45, 58; National Livestock & Meat Board: pp. 19, 21 (top); Reynolds Metals Co.: pp. 16-17, 33, 41, 60.

ISBN 0-89542-602-1 295

SANDWICH WREATH

20 party rye slices
20 party pumpernickel slices
  Butter or margarine

Spread bread with butter or margarine.
Spread half of bread slices with meat spread
mixture. Close sandwiches with remaining
slices. To form wreath, arrange sandwiches
around rim of a round plate. Decorate with a
velvet or satin bow.

DEVILED HAM SPREAD

1 4½-oz. can deviled ham
¼ c. chopped celery
½ t. Worcestershire sauce

Combine all ingredients.

CHICKEN SALAD SPREAD

1 4¾-oz. can chicken spread
¼ c. chopped apples
1 T. sour cream

Combine all ingredients.

Mrs. Peter Foley

3

HAM BALLS

1 lb. ground beef
1 lb. ground ham
2 eggs
1½ c. cracker crumbs
1 c. brown sugar
1 t. mustard
½ c. water
½ c. vinegar

Mix together first 4 ingredients and shape into balls. Combine remaining ingredients and pour over ham balls. Bake 1½ hours in a 300° oven.

Violet M. Witt

HOT CRABMEAT

1 8-oz. pkg. cream cheese
1 T. milk
6½ ozs. crabmeat
2 T. instant chopped onion
½ t. cream-style horseradish
½ t. salt
½ t. pepper

Soften cream cheese with the milk. Combine all ingredients in a baking dish. Bake at 375° for 15 minutes. Serve hot on crackers.

Adeline Ames

For a decorative centerpiece, fill a glass bowl with little paper fruits and small ornaments.

FRENCH-STYLE APPETIZER

1 12-oz. can luncheon meat
8 T. butter or margarine
½ t. tabasco
¼ c. minced parsley
1 clove garlic, minced
   (or 1 t. garlic powder)
1 pkg. party rye bread

Cut luncheon meat into thin 2-inch squares. Mix softened butter with tabasco, parsley, garlic. Spread thickly on bread. Top with luncheon meat. Cover with foil. Refrigerate until butter hardens. Serves 12.

HERBED DRUMSTICKS

1 c. crushed herb stuffing mix
⅔ c. grated parmesan cheese
¼ c. chopped parsley
1 clove garlic, minced
8 chicken drumsticks
⅓ c. melted butter

Wash and dry the drumsticks. Combine first 4 ingredients. Dip chicken in the melted butter, then roll in crumbs. Arrange chicken, skin side up, on greased baking pan. Sprinkle remaining butter and crumbs over chicken. Bake at 375° for about 1 hour. Do not turn chicken.

Florence Miller

BACON-CHESTNUT APPETIZERS

15 slices bacon, halved
30 canned water chestnuts

Wrap halved bacon slices around chestnuts. Fasten with toothpicks. Broil until bacon is done. Serves 30.

SMOKY BEEF DIP

2 c. cottage cheese
1 3½-oz. pkg. smoked sliced beef, finely chopped
1 T. minced onion
1 T. chopped parsley
Freshly ground pepper to taste

Beat cottage cheese until fairly smooth. Add beef, onion, parsley and pepper. Blend well. Serve with crisp vegetables such as carrot, green pepper and celery sticks.

CLAM DIP

1 8-oz. pkg. cream cheese
1 8-oz. can minced clams
1 T. mayonnaise
½ t. garlic salt
1 T. Worcestershire sauce
¼ t. seasoned salt

Mix all ingredients together, adding clam juice for consistency desired. Refrigerate. This dip can be made a week ahead and refrigerated for later use.

Mrs. Paul S. Tyler

CREAMY CHEESE BALL

(Pictured on cover)

1 8-oz. pkg. cream cheese, softened
2 c. (8 ozs.) crumbled blue cheese
⅓ c. flaked coconut
1 t. finely grated onion
1 t. Worcestershire sauce
¼ c. flaked coconut
¼ c. chopped pecans
¼ c. finely chopped parsley

Combine cheeses. Cream well. Blend in ⅓ cup coconut, the onion and Worcestershire sauce. Cover and chill at least 6 hours.

Before serving time, combine remaining ingredients on piece of waxed paper. Form cheese mixture into a ball and roll in the coconut, pecan, parsley mixture until completely covered. Place on a platter. Serve with crackers.

APPETIZER CHEESE TRAY

A simple cheese tray is one of the easiest of appetizers to create. Begin with a centerpiece of club cheese in its attractive brown crock. Surround with slices of tangy blue or smoky provolone.

Add cubes of m   uenster cheese. S   lar and colby   ss, add to a

Ga   ch as
rad   carrot
sti   sticks
add   al oc-
cas   in the
ch

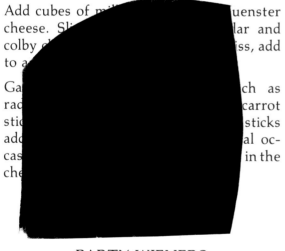

PARTY WIENERS

Frankfurters, Vienna sausages or cocktail wieners
⅓ c. prepared mustard
½ c. currant jelly

Cut meat in bite-size pieces. Mix mustard and jelly in 1-quart saucepan. Add meat. Cover and cook at low heat for 10 minutes. Serve on toothpicks with crackers. Makes ¾ cup sauce.

CHEESE BUDS

2 c. flour
½ lb. butter or margarine
½ lb. grated cheese
Salt and ground red pepper to taste

Soften cheese and butter and mix in with the flour. Season to taste. Pinch off small bits (does not raise) and place on a cookie sheet. Top with a pecan half. Bake at 400° approximately 15 minutes or until brown. Cool. Makes 60 cheese buds the size of a half dollar.

Mrs. Lee O. Dawkins

TOMATO TEASER

1 pt. cherry tomatoes
½ lb. bacon, cooked and crumbled
¼ t. tabasco

Cut out small hole in the top of each tomato. Combine crumbled bacon with tabasco. Spoon bacon mixture into tomatoes. Serve with food picks.

BEGINNER'S FONDUE

½ lb. American cheese, cubed
½ lb. colby cheese, cubed
1 c. milk
(or ¾ cup milk and ¼ cup white wine)

Combine above ingredients and cook over low heat, stirring often. Add milk or wine to thin when necessary.

For dunking, use cubed French bread, ham cubes, small meatballs, mushrooms, tiny onions, cauliflowerettes, large shell macaroni and wiener puffs.

Note: To make wiener puffs, cube wieners in ¾-inch pieces and bring to a boil in a little water. This will cause them to puff up.

Mrs. C. W. Anderson

BEVERAGES

TRADITIONAL EGGNOG

12 eggs, separated
1 c. sugar
1 qt. milk
2 c. bourbon
1 c. Jamaica rum
1 qt. heavy cream, whipped
  Nutmeg

Beat egg yolks slightly. Add sugar, a little at a time, and continue beating until smooth. Pour in milk, bourbon and rum and stir until well mixed. Beat egg whites until they stand in peaks. Fold egg whites and whipped cream into yolk mixture, gently but thoroughly. Serve cold with freshly grated nutmeg on top. Serves 25 to 30.

Virginia Kraegenbrink

FESTIVE PUNCH

1 pkg. fruit-flavored Kool-Aid
1½ c. sugar
1 small can unsweetened frozen
  orange juice
1 small can frozen pink lemonade

Put all ingredients in a gallon jar in order listed. Add water. Stir until dissolved.

Anne Krites

PUNCH CUBES

Juice of 2 lemons
Juice of 2 oranges
2 bananas, mashed
1 c. canned crushed pineapple
  and juice
¾ c. sugar
1 c. water

Combine above ingredients. (Place in blender for a few seconds if desired.) Pour into ice cube trays and freeze. Place three or four cubes in a glass and pour chilled ginger ale over cubes. Garnish with a maraschino cherry or mint leaves. Fills two trays.

Estella Long Black

HOT APRICOT GROG

1 46-oz. can apricot nectar
2 T. lemon juice
1½ c. brandy
  Lemon slices
  Whole cloves

Pour apricot nectar, lemon juice and brandy into a large pot. Bring to a simmer. Ladle into mugs or punch cups. Garnish each serving with a lemon slice stuffed with a clove. Makes 7½ cups.

WASSAIL

1½ c. sugar
4 c. boiling water
3 allspice berries
6 whole cloves
1 T. ground ginger
1 1-inch stick cinnamon
1⅓ c. orange juice
⅔ c. lemon juice

Combine sugar and 2 cups boiling water and boil 5 minutes. Add spices, cover and allow to stand 1 hour. Add remaining water and fruit juices and mix well. Strain. Heat to boiling point. Serve immediately. Makes about 1 quart.

CHRISTMAS CIDER

2 qts. apple cider
1 c. brown sugar
3 3-inch sticks cinnamon
1 t. whole cloves
1 t. salt

Heat cider to boiling point. Add remaining ingredients and simmer about 15 minutes. Strain and serve. Yield: 16 servings.

CRANBERRY PUNCH

- 4 c. cranberry juice
- 1½ c. sugar
- 4 c. pineapple juice
- 1 T. almond extract
- 2 qts. ginger ale

Combine first 4 ingredients. Stir until sugar ~~is dissolv~~ed. Chill. Then add ginger ale just ~~before s~~erving. Serves 30.

Mrs. N. C. Kitchin

Christmas Tree

OYSTER BISQUE

1 doz. shucked large raw oysters
1 c. oyster liquid
3 c. milk
1 c. heavy cream
1 slice onion
2 stalks celery
1 sprig parsley
1 bay leaf
⅓ c. butter or margarine, melted
⅓ c. flour
1¾ t. salt
½ t. tabasco
   Chopped chives

Drain oysters, reserving 1 cup liquid. Dice oysters into a saucepan and add liquid. Slowly bring oysters to boiling point, remove. In the same saucepan scald milk and cream with onion, celery, parsley, bay leaf. Strain. Blend butter with flour, salt and tabasco. Slowly stir in scalded milk. Stir over low heat until thick. Add oysters and cooking liquid. Heat. Garnish with chopped chives.

CREAM OF POTATO SOUP

5 large potatoes
½ c. sliced carrots
6 slices bacon
1 c. chopped onion
1 c. sliced celery
1½ t. salt
¼ t. white pepper
2 c. milk
2 c. light cream or evaporated milk
   Cheddar cheese, shredded
   Parsley

Wash, pare and slice potatoes. Cook with the carrots in boiling water to cover until tender. Drain. Sauté bacon until crisp. Drain on absorbent paper and crumble. Sauté onion and celery in 2 tablespoons of the bacon fat. Combine all ingredients except cheese and parsley. Simmer 30 minutes. Garnish each serving with cheddar cheese and parsley.

PIMIENTO BISQUE

2½ T. butter or margarine, melted
2½ T. flour
5 c. milk
½ t. grated onion
¾ c. pimiento
   Salt and pepper to taste

Add flour to melted butter. Mix well. Add milk and cook in a heavy saucepan, stirring constantly until thick. Add onion and coarsely sieved pimiento. Season to taste. Heat, stirring occasionally. Do not boil.

Mrs. William Lund

Beef Tingler

BEEF TINGLER

2 10½-oz. cans condensed beef broth
2 soup cans water
¼ c. brandy
¼ c. heavy cream
⅛ t. vanilla
   Dash of nutmeg
⅛ t. grated orange rind

In a saucepan, combine soup, water and brandy. Heat, stirring occasionally. Meanwhile, in a small bowl, combine cream, vanilla and nutmeg. Beat until cream just mounds. Fold in orange rind. Serve on soup. Makes 5½ cups.

JELLIED TOMATO SALAD

1 T. unflavored gelatin
¼ c. cold water
2½ c. fresh or canned tomatoes
1 T. minced onion
½ small bay leaf
½ t. sugar
½ t. salt
Pepper to taste
1 T. lemon juice
½ c. finely chopped cucumber
½ c. finely chopped celery
Lettuce or salad greens

Soften gelatin in the cold water. Cook tomatoes, onion and bay leaf (about 20 minutes for fresh tomatoes, 10 for canned). Press through a sieve and measure 1¾ cups (if not enough, add boiling water). Add hot, sieved tomatoes to gelatin and stir until gelatin is dissolved. Season with sugar, salt, pepper and lemon juice. Chill. When gelatin mixture begins to set, add cucumber and celery. Mix well. Pour into a mold or pan rinsed in cold water. Chill until firm. Serve with salad dressing on lettuce or salad greens. Serves 6.

Mrs. William Knox

TOSSED MUSHROOM SALAD

¼ lb. mushrooms, sliced
¼ c. lemon juice
1 head romaine lettuce
2 qts. chicory and escarole
2 to 3 heads endive

Arrange romaine leaves with ends up around the sides of a large salad bowl. In another bowl sprinkle mushrooms with lemon juice. Drain. Cut chicory and escarole in bite-size pieces and add with endive. Toss salad dressing with greens and place in salad bowl. Serves 12.

DRESSING

⅔ c. salad oil
½ c. tarragon vinegar
2 T. sugar
2 t. garlic salt
1 t. seasoned salt
¼ t. pepper

Combine all ingredients in a covered jar. Refrigerate approximately 30 minutes. Shake dressing to mix.

Judy Rodale

CHRISTMAS RIBBON SALAD

FIRST LAYER

2 3-oz. pkgs. lime gelatin
2½ c. hot water

Pour into a 9 x 13-inch enamel pan and let stand until firm in refrigerator.

SECOND LAYER

½ c. pineapple juice
20 large marshmallows, cut up

Heat above ingredients in a pan until the marshmallows melt. Dissolve 1 3-oz. package lemon gelatin in 1½ cups hot water.

Soften 1 8-oz. package cream cheese. Combine the hot marshmallow-pineapple liquid, gelatin and cream cheese and mix well. When cool, pour over the first layer and let stand in refrigerator.

THIRD LAYER

1 3-oz. pkg. cherry gelatin
1 3-oz. pkg. red raspberry gelatin
2½ c. hot water

Combine above ingredients. When cool, pour over the second layer and let stand until firm. Cut in 2- or 3-inch squares to serve.

Mrs. William C. Flick

SHRIMP SALAD LOUIS

1 c. mayonnaise
¼ c. French dressing
¼ c. catsup
1 t. horseradish
½ t. salt
1 t. Worcestershire sauce
½ t. tabasco
1 lb. cleaned and cooked shrimp
Shredded lettuce

Combine mayonnaise, French dressing, catsup, horseradish, salt, Worcestershire sauce, tabasco. Add shrimp, mix well. Serve on shredded lettuce. Makes 4 servings.

Note: One 7½-ounce can crabmeat may be added to shrimp in salad.

Gelatin Christmas Trees
Cranberry Stars
Christmas Wreath

CRANBERRY STARS

1 6-oz. pkg. cherry gelatin
3 c. boiling water
1 c. unconcentrated orange juice
1 c. crushed cranberries
½ c. finely diced celery
½ c. chopped pecans
Sour cream

Dissolve gelatin in the boiling water. Add juice. Stir and set aside to cool. Add cranberries and stir well. Then add celery and nuts. Pour into star-shaped molds. Refrigerate. When set unmold on lettuce leaves and top with 1 teaspoon sour cream.

Rebecca Temple Shelby

10

GELATIN CHRISTMAS TREES

1 3-oz. pkg. lime gelatin
1 envelope unflavored gelatin
1 c. boiling water
½ c. cold water
1 16-oz. can fruit cocktail
9 Lily pointed paper cups

Dissolve lime gelatin in the boiling water. Dissolve unflavored gelatin in the cold water. Add to first mixture and stir well. Add fruit cocktail, including juice, and stir. Cool at room temperature.

Rinse the pointed paper cups with water and place in 6-ounce frozen fruit cans or juice glasses, pointed side down. Pour cool gelatin mixture into cups and refrigerate. When ready to serve, unwrap paper cup with care (especially at tip). Place on salad plate. Surround with cottage cheese or sour cream.

Trees may be decorated with sour cream or whipped cream in a decorating tube if desired.

Dorothy G. Wofford

CAULIFLOWER SALAD

1 medium cauliflower
½ c. French dressing
1 small avocado, diced
½ c. sliced stuffed green olives
3 tomatoes, cut in eighths
½ c. roquefort cheese, crumbled
Crisp greens

Separate cauliflower into flowerettes. Cover with ice water and chill 1 hour. Drain. Break flowerettes into smaller pieces. Add dressing and let stand 2 hours. Just before serving add avocado, olives, tomatoes and cheese. Toss lightly. Serve on crisp greens. Serves 8.

Mrs. H. P. Clement

POINSETTIA SALAD

Arrange a few strips of pimiento on a slice of pineapple that has been placed on a lettuce leaf. Put a marshmallow in the center and top with a nutmeat. Serve with salad dressing.

Mrs. Solvei Slick

CHRISTMAS WREATH

1 20-oz. can sliced pineapple
1 3-oz. pkg. green gelatin
1 c. boiling water
1 16-oz. can whole berrry cranberry sauce
1 3-oz. pkg. red gelatin
1½ c. boiling water
1 c. heavy cream, whipped
1 c. salad dressing
Maraschino cherries

Drain pineapple, reserving syrup. Dissolve green gelatin in boiling water, and add syrup from pineapple. Pour into 6-cup ring mold. Place pineapple slices in mold, slightly overlapping and place a cherry in center of each slice. Chill until almost set. Dissolve red gelatin in boiling water and chill until partially set, then add cranberry sauce. Pour over green layer. Chill until firm. Unmold on serving platter.

Combine whipped cream and salad dressing. Place in center of mold.

Thin strips of pimiento or green pepper are good accents for salads.

CRANBERRY WHIPPED CREAM SALAD

1 8¼-oz. can crushed pineapple
1 3-oz. pkg. raspberry gelatin
1 16-oz. can whole cranberry sauce
1 t. grated orange peel
1 11-oz. can mandarin orange sections, drained
1 c. whipping cream, whipped

Drain pineapple, reserving the syrup. Add enough water to syrup to make 1 cup. Heat. Dissolve gelatin in this hot liquid. Stir in cranberry sauce and orange peel. Chill until partially set. Fold in mandarin oranges and pineapple. Fold whipped cream into fruit mixture. Pour into 6-cup mold. Chill until set. Unmold. Garnish with green grapes and cranberries rolled in egg white and lime- and raspberry-flavored gelatin. Serves 8 to 10.

Mrs. G. W. Furqueron

NOEL APPLE SALAD

6 apples
Dash of sugar
1 4-oz. jar green maraschino cherries
1 4-oz. jar red maraschino cherries
¾ c. walnuts
⅛ c. lemon juice
1½ c. dates
½ pt. sour cream

Partially peel apples, leaving some skin on for color. Then quarter and coarsely chop. Sprinkle lemon juice on apples to prevent apples from discoloring and toss thoroughly. In another bowl cut up the dates, cherries and nuts. Sprinkle apples with sugar. Refrigerate both bowls of fruit. Just before serving mix all together, adding as much sour cream as desired for dressing. Serve immediately.

Margaret H. De Hass

CREAMY FRUIT SALAD

1 8-oz. pkg. cream cheese
½ c. mayonnaise
½ pt. heavy cream, whipped
1 small can crushed pineapple, drained
1 bottle green cherries, drained
1 bottle red cherries, drained
2 c. miniature marshmallows
1 c. chopped walnuts

Cream together cream cheese and mayonnaise. Add fruit, marshmallows and nuts. Fold in whipped cream. Chill before serving.

Barbara Talbot Havens

FRUIT SALAD DRESSING

1 can sweetened condensed milk
2 whole eggs
½ t. dry mustard
½ t. salt
¾ c. vinegar

Put milk in a bowl. Add eggs, mustard and salt and beat slightly. Add vinegar and beat well. Store in refrigerator.

Mrs. A. W. Nutting

YULETIDE SALAD

1 3-oz. pkg. lemon gelatin
1 3-oz. pkg. pineapple gelatin
1 3-oz. pkg. strawberry gelatin
½ lb. marshmallows
½ pt. mayonnaise
½ pt. whipping cream, whipped
1 8-oz. pkg. cream cheese
2½ c. crushed pineapple, drained
1 small jar maraschino cherries, cut fine

Add pineapple juice to hot water in preparation of lemon and pineapple gelatin, making 4 cups of liquid. Stir in marshmallows and cool. Add cream cheese, mayonnaise, crushed pineapple and cherries to the whipped cream. Then combine with cooled gelatin. Pour in dish to set. Prepare strawberry gelatin according to directions on package. Cool, then use to top mixture in dish.

Mrs. Paul H. Betz

PURPLE LADY SALAD

2 3-oz. pkgs. strawberry gelatin
1 c. boiling water
1 small can crushed pineapple
1 can blueberries in heavy syrup
1 chopped banana (optional)
½ c. chopped nuts
½ pt. whipped topping

Dissolve gelatin in boiling water. Add pineapple and blueberries. (Do not drain.) Let set in refrigerator until thick. Fold in whipped topping and nuts.

Mrs. T. B. Henry

STUFFED MUSHROOMS

1½ lbs. large fresh mushrooms
½ c. butter or margarine
3 T. finely chopped green onions
2 slices fresh bread, crumbled
½ c. chopped parsley
1 t. leaf savory, crumbled
Salt and pepper to taste

Remove mushroom stems, chop fine. Melt ¼ cup of the butter or margarine in a skillet. Sauté mushroom caps on both sides until beige in color. Place in a pan. Melt remaining butter. Sauté mushroom stems and onions briefly. Remove from heat. Add remaining ingredients. Toss lightly. Spoon into mushroom caps. Bake at 350° for 20 minutes, or until tender.

Mrs. J. P. Parks

CREAMED CELERY WITH ALMONDS

4 c. celery, sliced in ½ inch pieces
1 10½-oz. can condensed cream of celery soup
½ c. milk
1 t. instant minced onion
1 T. finely chopped parsley or chives
1 T. finely chopped pimiento
½ c. toasted diced almonds

Cook celery in boiling salted water for 5 minutes. Drain. Combine next 5 ingredients, then the celery. Pour into a 1½-quart casserole. Sprinkle almonds over top. Bake at 350° for 20 minutes or until heated through and lightly browned.

COTTAGE CHEESE-ASPARAGUS MOUSSE

1 envelope unflavored gelatin
¼ c. water
1 14½-oz. can cut green asparagus spears, drained
1½ c. cottage cheese, sieved
2 T. lemon juice
½ t. prepared mustard
½ t. salt
1 c. chopped blanched almonds

Sprinkle gelatin over water to soften. Drain asparagus, reserving liquid. Add enough water to make 1 cup. In a 1-quart saucepan, heat liquid to boiling. Stir in softened gelatin until dissolved. Cool slightly. In a bowl combine cottage cheese, lemon juice, mustard, salt, almonds and asparagus. Add gelatin mixture. Turn into 4-cup salad mold. Chill until firm. Unmold on salad greens. Serves 6 to 8.

HERBED CUCUMBERS

2 T. salad oil
1 t. salt
2 cucumbers, thinly sliced
1 small onion, sliced
2 T. water
½ t. tabasco
2 T. chopped fresh thyme

Heat oil with salt in a skillet. Add cucumbers and onion. Cook over medium heat, stirring constantly, about 3 minutes. Add water, tabasco and thyme. Cover. Cook, shaking skillet occasionally, about 2 minutes or until barely tender. Serves 4.

MINTED PEAS

1 20-oz. can peas, drained
½ t. salt
¼ t. pepper
1 T. margarine
⅓ c. mint jelly

Cook liquid from peas until ¼ cup remains. Add rest of ingredients. Simmer and serve.

BROCCOLI WITH STUFFING

- 2 pkgs. frozen broccoli
- 2 eggs, beaten
- 1 onion, chopped fine
- 1 can mushroom soup
- ½ c. mayonnaise
- 1 c. grated cheddar cheese
- ¼ c. melted butter or margarine
- 1 pkg. herbed stuffing mix

Cook broccoli. Combine eggs, onion, soup and mayonnaise. Place layer of broccoli in a 2-quart casserole. Add layer of cheese. Pour small amount of sauce on top. Repeat layers until all are used. Top with stuffing mix. Sprinkle butter or margarine on top. Bake for 30 minutes at 350°.

Mrs. Kenneth Zebley

- 6 medium sweet potatoes
- ½ c. margarine
- 1 c. brown sugar
- 1 c. pecans or walnuts, chopped
- 2 c. cornflakes, crushed
- 12 marshmallows

Boil potatoes, peel and mash. Mix well with margarine, sugar and nuts. Form a ball around one large marshmallow, then roll in crushed cornflakes. Just before serving, warm balls in a 350° oven about 15 minutes or until marshmallow has softened or melted.

These balls may be made ahead of time and refrigerated or frozen for later use. Makes 12 balls.

Lucille Pearces

SQUASH PUFFS

1 qt. frozen yellow squash
¼ c. milk
3 T. flour
1 T. light brown sugar
½ t. salt
½ t. ground nutmeg
⅛ t. ground black pepper
2 large eggs, beaten

Place squash in a saucepan with ½ cup water and ½ teaspoon salt. Cook until tender (1 quart should yield about 3 cups, cooked). Combine squash with remaining ingredients and mix well. Place into buttered 1-quart casserole. Bake at 350° for 35 minutes. Serves 6.

Rosy Meier

CANDIED SWEET POTATOES

2 1-lb. cans sweet potatoes,
  halved or quartered
1 c. orange juice
2 T. melted butter
½ c. white sugar
½ c. brown sugar
1 T. cornstarch

Mix all ingredients together except the potatoes. Pour mixture over potatoes in a greased casserole. Bake 1 hour at 325°. Or prepare syrup on top of stove, add potatoes and cook a few minutes.

Mrs. James F. Bateman

DELICIOUS POTATOES

1½ c. milk
½ c. butter or margarine
6 medium-size potatoes
¼ green pepper
¼ sweet red pepper (or ¼ c. pimiento)
5 green onions with about
  3 inches of green
1 t. salt

Preheat oven to 200° to 250°. Melt butter or margarine in the milk. Do not boil. Grate or grind potatoes, peppers and onions. Put into a 1½-quart casserole. Add salt. Pour on milk. Bake 4 to 6 hours. Add more milk if necessary. Fry leftovers for breakfast.

Alma Toth

GLAZED CARROTS

3 c. cooked carrots
⅓ c. sugar
1 T. flour
2 t. grated orange rind
¾ c. orange juice

Mix sugar and flour. Add orange rind and juice. Cook over low heat until thick. Pour over carrots.

Mrs. R. C. Sauer

FRUITED RICE

1 c. sliced carrots
3 T. vegetable oil
1 c. sliced green onions
2 c. sliced, cored unpeeled apples
3 c. cooked brown rice
1 t. salt
½ c. seedless raisins
1 T. sesame seeds

Sauté carrots in the oil about 10 minutes. Add onions and apples. Cook 10 more minutes. Stir in rice, salt and raisins. Cook, stirring constantly, until rice is heated through. Add sesame seeds and toss lightly. Serves 6.

FRENCH FRIED CAULIFLOWER

1 large head cauliflower
1 egg, slightly beaten
1 c. milk
1 T. melted fat
1 c. enriched flour

Break cauliflower into flowerettes. Cook in small amount of boiling water 5 minutes. Combine egg, milk and fat. Gradually add to sifted dry ingredients, beat smooth. Dip cauliflower into batter. Fry in deep, hot fat until golden brown. Takes 2 to 3 minutes.

Mrs. Paul E. King

BEETS RUSSE

2 c. hot cubed beets
½ c. French dressing
½ c. minced green onion
1 c. sour cream, whipped

Mix beets with dressing. Place in serving dish. Top with sour cream. Sprinkle with minced onion.

Mrs. Kenneth L. Gray

CASSEROLES

SWEET POTATO CASSEROLE

3 medium sweet potatoes
½ c. margarine
1 c. brown sugar
⅛ t. cinnamon
⅛ t. nutmeg
1 t. salt
Milk

Cook potatoes until tender. Drain. Add margarine, brown sugar and enough milk to make soupy. Add cinnamon, nutmeg and salt. Mix and place in a casserole.

TOPPING

¼ stick margarine
½ c. sugar
⅛ c. milk
1 t. vanilla
½ c. toasted salted pecans

Melt margarine, sugar and milk. Cook until thick and bubbly. Cool. Add vanilla and beat well. Put mixture over potatoes. Sprinkle with nuts. Reheat at 400° until bubbly. Serves 6 to 8.

Mrs. G. A. Hoffman

ENGLISH PEA AND CHESTNUT CASSEROLE

½ c. butter
1 small onion, minced
2 T. chopped green pepper
1 c. sliced celery
2 cans English peas, drained
1 can water chestnuts, sliced
2 diced pimientos
1 can cream of mushroom soup, undiluted
Buttered cracker crumbs

Melt butter in a heavy skillet. Add onion, green pepper and celery. Sauté over medium heat, stirring often until soft. Remove from heat and add peas and chestnuts. Fold in pimientos. Arrange a layer of the vegetable mixture in bottom of a 2-quart buttered casserole. Top with undiluted soup. Repeat layer. Sprinkle with buttered cracker crumbs. Bake at 350° for 30 minutes.

Mrs. Robert L. Duggins

Flemish Beef Casserole

FLEMISH BEEF CASSEROLE

1½ lbs. onions, thinly sliced
2 cloves garlic, minced
¾ c. vegetable oil, divided
4 lbs. round steak, cubed
¼ c. flour
  Salt and pepper to taste
4 sprigs parsley
½ t. nutmeg
½ t. thyme leaves
2 bay leaves
2 12-oz. cans beer

Sauté onions and garlic in ¼ cup oil until transparent. Remove from pan. Trim fat from meat. Dredge meat in flour mixed with 2 teaspoons salt and a dash of pepper. Add remaining oil to pan and brown meat well on all sides. Line two 2-quart casseroles with heavy-duty aluminum foil. Divide ingredients between the two casseroles. Place meat on bottom, spread onions and parsley over top. Sprinkle with remaining herbs. Top with beer and an additional ½ teaspoon salt over each casserole. Cover casserole with aluminum foil. Cook in preheated 325° oven about 2 hours, or until meat is tender. Serve one casserole, cool and freeze the other. Makes two 2-quart casseroles.

CORN BAKE

3 1-lb. cans whole kernel corn, drained
1 c. milk
2 eggs
½ c. ground ham
¼ c. ground cheese
1 slice ground bread
2 T. onion, finely chopped (optional)
  Salt and pepper to taste

Mix above ingredients together and pour into a greased 10 x 6 x 1½-inch baking pan. Mix 1½ cups bread (cubed) with 2 or 3 tablespoons melted butter and place on top of corn mixture. Sprinkle with 1 tablespoon grated parmesan cheese. Place pan on a cookie sheet and bake at 350° for 25 minutes. Serves 7.

Chopped peppers may also be used for added color and flavor if desired.

Glad Leonard

MEATS

PORK STEAKS WITH APPLE STUFFING

6 pork steaks, ½-inch thick
2 T. fat
3 tart red apples, cored and halved
Salt and pepper to taste

Slowly brown pork steaks on both sides in hot fat. Season well with salt and pepper. Place in shallow baking dish. Cover each steak with a layer of the following apple stuffing; top with apple half. Sprinkle with sugar. Cover dish tightly with foil. Bake at 350° for 1 hour or until pork is well done.

APPLE STUFFING

3 c. toasted bread crumbs
1½ c. chopped unpared apples
½ c. seedless raisins
½ c. chopped celery
½ c. chopped onion
1 t. salt
1 t. poultry seasoning
¼ t. pepper
½ c. canned condensed beef broth

Combine all ingredients except beef broth. Add broth and toss lightly just enough to moisten.

ORANGE-GINGER PORK CHOPS

6 lean pork chops
¼ c. orange juice
½ t. salt
1 t. ground ginger
6 orange slices (1 large orange)
¾ c. dairy sour cream

In a skillet brown chops well over medium heat, about 10 minutes per side. Add orange juice, cover and simmer about 30 minutes. Uncover, sprinkle chops with salt and ginger and top each with an orange slice. Cover and cook 10 to 15 minutes more or until chops are fork tender. Remove chops to an oven-proof platter and top each with sour cream. Place under broiler about 1 minute. Serve immediately.

Carol P. Wells

SLICED BEEF IN ONION SAUCE

1 lb. chuck, shoulder or round, cut in ¼-inch slices (cross-grained)
1½ t. salt
Dash of pepper
3 T. shortening
1 c. water
½ lb. large onions, cut into thick slices
2 T. flour
1 t. sugar

Season meat with salt and pepper. Brown on both sides in melted shortening. Add ¼ cup of the water and cover tightly. Simmer gently 1 to 1½ hours, or until meat is tender. Add remaining water a ¼ cup at a time to keep pan from drying out. Push meat to one side of pan and carefully place onions in the juice. Cover. Simmer ½ hour or longer until onions are transparent and tender. Transfer meat and onions to hot platter and cover. Stir combined sugar and flour into juice, adding more water if desired. Heat to boiling and pour over meat and onions. Serve at once. Yield: 4 servings.

Pat Philley

INDIVIDUAL HAM LOAVES

1 lb. ground ham
½ lb. ground lean pork
½ lb. ground lean beef
1 c. fine cracker crumbs
2 T. chopped onion
2 T. chopped celery
2 T. chopped green pepper
½ t. salt
¼ t. pepper
2 eggs, beaten
1 c. milk

Combine above ingredients in order listed. Shape into 10 or 12 loaves. Arrange in a baking dish with the following sauce. Bake in a 350° oven for 50 to 60 minutes. Baste often.

SAUCE

1 8-oz. can tomato sauce
3 T. vinegar
1 t. dry mustard
1 c. firmly packed brown sugar

Combine all ingredients.

Mrs. Robert M. Black

BEEF RIB ROAST

1 3- to 4-rib beef rib roast

To make carving easier, have butcher loosen back (chine) bone by sawing across ribs. Tie roast. Place roast, fat side up, on a rack in an open roasting pan. Insert meat thermometer so bulb is centered in the thickest part of roast. Do not add water. Do not cover. Roast in a 325° oven to desired degree of doneness. The meat thermometer will register 140° for rare, 160° for medium and 170° for well done. For a 4- to 6-pound roast, allow 26 to 32 minutes per pound for rare, 34 to 38 minutes for medium and 40 to 42 for well done. For a 6- to 8-pound roast, allow 23 to 25 minutes per pound for rare, 27 to 30 for medium and 32 to 35 for well done. For easier carving, allow roast to stand in a warm place 15 to 20 minutes after removal from oven. Since roasts usually continue to cook after removal from oven, it is best to remove them when the thermometer registers about 5° below the temperature of doneness desired. Before carving roast, remove strings. With a sharp knife, remove backbone and feather bones from roast.

WALNUT-STUFFED BEEF ROLLS

- 2 1-lb. top round steaks, ½-inch thick
- ¼ c. flour
- ½ c. butter or margarine
- ⅓ c. onion, chopped
- ⅓ c. celery, chopped
- 2 c. bread cubes
- ⅔ c. walnuts, chopped
- ⅓ c. parsley
- 1 t. salt
- 1 egg
- 1⅓ c. water
- 2 10-oz. pkgs. Brussels sprouts
- 1 10¾-oz. can beef gravy

Cut each steak crosswise into 3 uniform pieces. Sprinkle with flour. Pound each side until steaks are ¼-inch thick. Cook onion and celery in ¼ cup of the butter or margarine until tender, 4 to 5 minutes. Add bread cubes, nuts, parsley and salt. Cook until bread is lightly browned. Remove from heat. Stir in egg.

Spread each piece of meat with walnut mixture, leaving ½ inch around edges. Roll up and secure with toothpicks. Place 4 tablespoons margarine or butter in a large skillet. Brown beef rolls well on all sides. Add ⅔ cup water. Reduce heat to low and simmer, covered, 30 minutes, stirring occasionally. Add Brussels sprouts, beef gravy and remaining water. Heat to boiling. Cover and cook 10 minutes. Serves 6.

Mrs. James Carter

FROSTED MEAT LOAF

- 1½ lbs. ground beef
- 1 can mushroom soup
- 1 c. small bread cubes
- ¼ c. chopped onion
- 1 egg, beaten
- ½ t. salt
  Dash of pepper
- 2 c. mashed potatoes
- ¼ c. water
- 1 T. drippings

Mix thoroughly ground beef, ½ cup of the soup, bread cubes, onion, egg and seasoning. Shape into a loaf. Place in shallow baking pan. Bake at 350° for 1 hour. Frost loaf with potatoes. Bake 15 more minutes. Blend remaining soup, the water and drippings. Heat. Serve with meat.

Andrea L. Dodd

GOURMET MEAT ROLL

- 2 eggs, beaten
- ¾ c. soft bread crumbs
- ½ c. tomato juice
- ¼ c. sherry
- 2 T. chopped parsley
- 1 small clove garlic, chopped
- ½ t. salt
- ¼ t. pepper
- 2 lbs. ground beef
- 8 thin slices boiled ham
- 1½ c. shredded mozzarella cheese
- 3 slices mozzarella cheese, halved diagonally

Combine eggs, bread crumbs, tomato juice, sherry, parsley, garlic, salt and pepper. Stir in ground beef, mixing well. On foil or waxed paper, pat meat to a 12 x 10-inch rectangle. Arrange ham slices on top of meat, leaving a small margin around edges. Sprinkle shredded cheese over ham. Starting from short end, roll up meat, using foil to lift. Seal edges and ends. Place roll seam-side-down in a 13 x 9 x 2-inch pan. Bake in a 350° oven for 1 hour and 15 minutes. Place cheese wedges over top of roll, return to oven for 5 minutes until cheese melts. Serves 8.

Laura Pessagno

BEEF PIQUANT IN RICE RING

- 1½ lbs. tenderized round steak, cut in 1-inch strips
- 2 T. chili powder
- 2 t. salt
- ½ t. garlic powder
- 4 c. hot cooked rice
- 1 t. onion powder
- 1 c. cooked seasoned green peas
- 2 T. chopped parsley
- 2 T. vegetable oil
- 1 8-oz. can tomato sauce

Season beef strips with chili powder, salt and garlic powder. Let meat stand about 30 minutes to absorb the flavor of the spices.

Combine rice, onion powder, green peas and parsley. Toss gently. Pack into a 1½-quart ring mold. Cover and place mold in a pan of hot water until serving time. Sauté steak in hot oil about 10 minutes. Add tomato sauce. Cover and cook 10 minutes longer. Invert rice ring on heated platter. Fill ring with meat mixture. Makes 6 servings.

BAKED BONELESS SMOKED HAM

1 5- to 7-lb. smoked boneless ham

Place ham, lean side down, on a rack in an open roasting pan. Insert roast meat thermometer so that the bulb is centered in the thickest part. Do not add water. Do not cover. Roast in a 325° oven, allowing 15 to 18 minutes per pound. For a fully cooked ham weighing 6 pounds, this will take approximately 1¾ hours.

Prepare the following sauce. During the last 30 minutes of cooking time, brush ham with ½ cup of the sauce. Serve remaining sauce hot with ham.

ORANGE-RAISIN SAUCE

- ¼ c. raisins
- 2 c. orange juice
- 2 T. cornstarch
- 2 T. water
- ½ t. salt
- 1 T. prepared mustard

Place raisins and orange juice in a saucepan. Bring to a simmer, cover and cook slowly 10 minutes. Combine cornstarch, water, salt and mustard. Stir into first mixture. Cook, stirring constantly, until thickened.

SPICY JELLY-GLAZED PORK ROAST

- 1 4- to 5-lb. pork loin roast
- 1 t. salt
- ½ t. allspice
- ½ c. currant or apple jelly
- ¼ c. light corn syrup
- 3 T. catsup
  Canned or fresh pineapple and orange slices
  Watercress, mint sprigs or parsley

Rub outside of roast with salt and ¼ teaspoon allspice. Place roast on a rack in a shallow uncovered baking pan. If meat thermometer is used, insert point in center of lean part of loin away from bone. Roast in 325° oven until done, 2¾ to 3 hours, or to an internal temperature of 170° if a meat thermometer is used. Prepare glaze while meat is roasting. Combine jelly, syrup, catsup and remaining allspice in a saucepan. Simmer 2 minutes. Brush meat with sauce several times during last 30 minutes of roasting. If desired, garnish with canned or fresh pineapple and orange slices and watercress, mint sprigs or parsley. Yield: 6 to 8 servings.

POULTRY

DUCKLING A L'ANGLAISE

1 4- to 5-lb. duckling
Salt and pepper to taste
3 c. bread crumbs
1 T. onion, minced
¼ c. celery, chopped fine
Thyme to taste

Prepare duck for roasting and rub with salt. Combine remaining ingredients and stuff duckling. Sew securely. Rub outside with softened butter and place in a shallow pan. Bake at 375°. Allow 30 to 35 minutes per pound.

Serve with carrots, cauliflower, boiled potatoes and cranberry sauce.

Mrs. Chester Arlington

ROAST TURKEY

1 10- to 12-lb. turkey
8 c. stuffing
1 c. melted butter or margarine

Preheat oven to 325°. Fill dressed, cleaned bird with stuffing. Skewer or sew openings. Truss and arrange on a rack in a shallow roasting pan. Roast, uncovered, until tender, 3½ to 4 hours. When turkey begins to brown, cover lightly with a tent of aluminum foil. Remove foil and baste occasionally with butter during roasting.

WILD RICE STUFFING

1 c. raw wild rice
3 c. chicken broth or bouillon
1 c. diced celery
¼ c. minced onion
½ c. melted butter
1 4-oz. can mushrooms
½ t. salt
¼ t. pepper
¼ t. sage

Add rice to boiling broth. Cover and let simmer slowly 30 to 45 minutes until broth is absorbed. Sauté celery and onion in butter 2 or 3 minutes. Combine all ingredients. Stuffing is enough for a 10-pound turkey.

Adeline Roseberg

HOLIDAY DUCK

1 4½- to 5-lb. duckling
Salt
⅔ c. orange marmalade
½ c. barbecue sauce

Salt duckling, then place on a rack in a shallow roasting pan, breast side up. Cover loosely with aluminum foil and bake at 425° for 45 minutes. Prick skin occasionally. Reduce heat to 325° and bake 1½ hours. Pour off drippings and remove foil. Continue roasting 45 minutes to 1 hour, or until tender. Brush often with a mixture of the orange marmalade and barbecue sauce. Serve on rice if desired.

Mrs. P. E. Edwards

Andrea Kerry Shafer

ROAST GOOSE WITH APPLES

1 8-lb. goose
2 c. bread crumbs
1 chopped onion
2 T. fat
¼ t. sage
1 t. salt
Pinch of pepper
6 to 8 apples
¼ c. brown sugar
3 sweet potatoes

Cook giblets until tender. Chop and add to stuffing made by mixing bread crumbs, onion, fat, sage and seasoning. After cleaning the goose thoroughly, stuff and sew the neck and back. Roast 15 minutes at 500°, then reduce heat to 350° and cook 3 hours. Wash and core apples. Sprinkle with brown sugar, stuff with mashed and seasoned sweet potatoes. Bake until tender and serve hot with the goose.

Photograph opposite
Roast Goose

CHICKEN NEWBURG

⅓ c. butter
¼ c. flour
2 c. milk
¾ c. shredded cheddar cheese
1 T. chopped pimiento
1 t. salt
½ c. toasted slivered almonds
½ c. sliced fresh mushrooms
1½ c. cooked sliced chicken
¼ c. cooking sherry
1 t. minced onion
¼ t. pepper

Melt butter and sauté mushrooms for 2 minutes in a chafing dish. Stir in flour until smooth. Add milk, stirring constantly. Add chicken and remaining ingredients, except almonds. Top with almonds just before serving. Serve with rice or patty shells.

Mitzie Turck

GLAZED CHICKEN

1 frying chicken, quartered
½ c. butter
1½ t. salt
1 c. plum jam
1 T. catsup
2 t. grated lemon rind
5 t. lemon juice

Melt butter. Add chicken, browning on both sides. Add salt. Put meat in a shallow baking pan. Combine remaining ingredients and pour over chicken. Bake in a preheated 375° oven about 30 to 40 minutes.

Mrs. William Hoode

POULTRY DRESSING

5 c. seasoned bread cubes
2 eggs, beaten
2½ c. cut-up chicken
2 c. chicken broth
1 can cream of mushroom soup
½ c. milk
¼ c. butter

Heat broth, soup, milk and butter until butter melts. Pour over bread cubes, then mix in eggs and chicken. Put in a bean pot. Bake at 350° for 35 minutes.

Janice Prause

SPICY CHICKEN

1 c. plain yogurt
1½ t. salt
1 small clove garlic, crushed
½ t. ground cardamom
½ t. chili powder
¼ t. cinnamon
¼ t. ginger
1 2½- to 3-lb. broiler-fryer chicken, quartered
2 t. flour

In a small bowl combine first 7 ingredients. In a shallow dish marinate chicken in the yogurt mixture at least 4 hours or overnight. Place chicken skin side up in a baking pan. Combine flour with marinade. Spoon on chicken. Bake in a preheated 350° oven about 1½ hours or until tender, basting occasionally with the marinade.

CHICKEN KIEV

½ c. plus 2 T. butter or margarine
2 T. chopped parsley
1 clove garlic, minced
¼ t. rosemary, crushed
   Dash of pepper
3 chicken breasts (2½ lbs.), split, skinned, boned
1 egg, slightly beaten
½ c. fine dry bread crumbs
2 T. chopped onion
1 10½-oz. can condensed cream of chicken soup
⅓ c. milk
2 T. sherry

Blend together ½ cup butter, 1 tablespoon parsley, garlic, rosemary and seasoning. Form a patty ¾-inch thick. Freeze until firm. Flatten chicken with edge of heavy saucer to ¼-inch thick. Cut butter into 6 equal pieces. Place one in center of each breast. Tuck in ends and roll tightly. Secure with toothpicks. Dip in egg and then in bread crumbs. Chill.

In a saucepan, cook onion with the remaining parsley in the 2 tablespoons butter until tender. Blend in remaining ingredients. Heat, stirring occasionally. Fry two chicken rolls at a time in deep fat at 350° for 10 to 12 minutes until well browned. Drain. Serve with sauce.

Roberta M. Allen

CRANBERRY CASSEROLE BREAD

- 2 c. flour
- ¾ c. sugar
- 2 t. baking powder
- ½ t. baking soda
- 1 t. salt
- ¼ c. shortening
- ¾ c. orange juice
- 1 T. grated orange rind
- 2 eggs, well beaten
- 1 c. coarsely chopped cranberries
- ½ c. chopped glacé green cherries

Stir flour, sugar, baking powder, baking soda and salt together. Cut in shortening until mixture resembles coarse cornmeal. Combine orange juice and grated rind with eggs. Pour all at once into dry ingredients, mixing just enough to dampen. Dust chopped cranberries and cherries with a tablespoon of flour, then carefully fold into batter. Spoon into a well-greased 1½-quart casserole. Bake in a 350° oven about 1 hour, or until a toothpick inserted in center comes out clean. Cool 10 minutes. Frost with a confectioners' sugar icing.

Mary Wasco

CONFECTIONERS' SUGAR FROSTING

- 3 T. margarine
- 2 c. confectioners' sugar
- ⅛ t. salt
- 1 t. vanilla
- 3 T. warm milk

Cream margarine. Add salt and sugar and mix thoroughly. Add milk and vanilla and beat until fluffy.

SWEET FRUIT LOAF

- 1 pkg. granular yeast
- ½ c. lukewarm water
- ½ t. salt
- ¼ c. sugar
- ½ c. lukewarm water
- 1 egg, beaten
- ¼ c. melted shortening
- 2 c. plus 2 T. sifted all-purpose flour
- ½ t. nutmeg
- 1 c. fruit mix (chopped raisins and chopped glacé cherries)

Soften yeast in ½ cup lukewarm water. Add the next four ingredients and beat well. Add shortening, then flour and spice. Beat well. Fold in fruit mix. Let rise until double in bulk. Beat again. Put into greased bread tin. Let rise again until almost double in bulk. Bake 45 minutes in a 375° oven.

Lillian H. Gray

BUTTERHORNS

- 1 c. butter
- ½ c. sugar
- 2 eggs, beaten
- 1 c. warm milk
- 2 envelopes dry yeast
- 4½ c. flour
- ½ t. salt

Dissolve yeast in part of the warm milk. Add to rest of ingredients. (Before adding all of the flour, add only enough to form a light sponge dough. Beat this with an electric mixer until well blended. Then add rest of flour or enough to make dough stiff enough to handle.) Knead 10 minutes. Place in greased bowl and grease top of dough. Cover and let rise until double in bulk. Roll dough, then brush with melted butter. Cut in pie-shaped wedges and roll each piece, starting from the wide edge. Place on a greased cookie sheet or pan, turn each to form a crescent shape, brush with shortening, cover and let rise until double. Bake in a 375° oven about 20 minutes or until lightly browned. While still warm frost with a confectioners' sugar icing to which almond or orange extract has been added. Top with finely chopped nuts.

Mrs. Oscar Schaubs

SWISS CHRISTMAS BREAD

5 c. sifted flour
2 pkgs. active dry yeast
1 c. milk, scalded
½ c. hot tap water
¼ c. sugar
1 t. salt
½ t. nutmeg
½ t. mace
¼ t. cloves
1 egg
¼ c. butter, melted
½ c. raisins
½ c. cut candied cherries
¼ c. cut citron
¼ c. chopped nuts

Combine 2 cups of the flour with the yeast in a bowl. Cool milk to lukewarm. Blend yeast mixture, milk and next 7 ingredients and mix. Beat with a beater about 3 minutes. Add remaining ingredients. Mix. Add remaining flour gradually and knead until smooth. Place in a lightly greased bowl. Grease surface of dough lightly. Cover and let rise in a warm place until double in bulk, about 30 minutes. Turn out on a lightly floured board. Punch down, divide into 2 equal parts and mold each part into a loaf. Put each loaf into a greased 8½ x 4½ x 2½-inch pan. Cover. Let rise in a warm place until double in bulk, about 30 minutes. Bake in a preheated 375° oven about 40 minutes.

PUMPKIN BREAD

2⅔ c. sugar
⅔ c. shortening
4 eggs, beaten
⅔ c. water
2 c. pumpkin
3½ c. flour
½ t. baking powder
2 t. baking soda
1½ t. salt
1 t. cinnamon
½ t. cloves
⅔ c. nuts
⅔ c. raisins
⅔ c. chopped dates

Combine sugar and shortening, add eggs, water and pumpkin. Sift dry ingredients and combine with first mixture. Add nuts, raisins and dates. Bake for 1 hour at 350°. Makes 2 loaves.

Elaine Nelson

CHRISTMAS STOLLEN

1 pkg. granulated yeast
¼ c. warm water
¼ c. sugar
½ t. salt
¼ c. butter
1 egg
¼ c. milk
2¼ c. sifted flour
1 c. candied fruit mix
2 c. sifted confectioners' sugar
3 T. warm milk or cream
1 T. melted butter
½ t. vanilla or lemon extract
Red and green candied cherries
Multicolored candied fruit pieces

Dissolve yeast in warm water. Cream sugar, salt and butter. Add egg and milk, beating well. Blend in ½ cup of the flour and let stand for a few minutes. Stir in dissolved yeast and water mixture. Beat in remaining flour and turn out onto a lightly floured board. Cover dough with a clean dish towel and let set for 10 minutes, then remove towel and knead the dough until it is light and smooth. (Butter your hands if necessary to keep dough from sticking.) Place dough in a large, well-buttered bowl and cover with a towel. Allow dough to rise until double in bulk, approximately 1½ hours. Punch dough down and let rise again until almost double in bulk, 30 to 45 minutes. Remove dough from bowl and divide in half. Place on a lightly floured board and let stand for 10 minutes. Flatten dough mounds and knead ½ cup candied fruit into each mound. Flatten into two ovals and fold each over the long way, pressing edges firmly together so they cannot spring open while baking.

Mold each into a crescent shape and place on a lightly buttered, heavy baking sheet. Brush tops with melted butter, cover with towel and let rise until double in bulk, 35 to 45 minutes. Bake on center rack in 375° oven from 30 to 35 minutes. Frost while warm with a confectioners' sugar icing. Decorate icing with whole candied cherries and multicolored candied fruit pieces.

Jacqueline Shafer

CAKES

TOFFEE CAKE

½ c. butter
2 c. flour
1 c. brown sugar
½ c. white sugar
1 c. buttermilk
1 t. baking soda
1 egg
1 t. vanilla

Blend flour, butter, sugars. Set aside ½ cup of the mixture. To remaining mixture add buttermilk, soda, egg and vanilla. Blend well. Pour into a greased 10 x 14-inch pan.

TOPPING

6 chocolate toffee bars
½ c. pecans

Crush finely candy bars and nuts. Add to the ½ cup of reserved mixture. Sprinkle over batter. Bake at 350° for 40 minutes.

Cheryl J. Wachsmuth

HOT MILK CAKE

1 c. milk
⅛ lb. butter
2 c. sugar
4 eggs
2 t. baking powder
2 c. flour
1 t. vanilla

Heat milk and butter in a saucepan until butter melts. Beat sugar and eggs until creamy. Add baking powder and flour to the sugar and egg mixture, then add milk and butter. Mix. Add vanilla. Bake in a tube pan at 325° to 350° for 30 minutes. Do not peek in the oven during this period. Bake 15 to 20 minutes longer. Test for doneness by inserting toothpick in center of cake. Ice with the following:

ICING

1 8-oz. pkg. cream cheese
½ c. margarine
1 lb. confectioners' sugar

Blend cream cheese and margarine. Add sugar. Color with a few drops of red or green food coloring.

Barbara J. Hoffman

The 12 x 10-inch see-through folding book viewer stand protects cookbooks from smudges and dirt. It folds flat for storage or hanging. See page 64 for more information.

WHIPPED CREAM CAKE

1 c. sugar
3 egg whites, stiffly beaten
1 c. whipping cream, whipped
¼ t. salt
2 c. flour
2 t. baking powder
½ c. water
1 t. vanilla

Fold whipped cream into stiffly beaten egg whites. Sift salt, flour, sugar and baking powder 3 times and add alternately with water and vanilla. Bake in a 350° oven in a medium-size loaf pan for about ½ hour. If desired, add ½ cup chopped black walnuts with the vanilla.

Mary Alice Campbell

CRANBERRY CAKE

1 pkg. yellow cake mix
1 pkg. fluffy white frosting mix

Make cake as directed on package. When cool, cut the layers in half so there will be four pieces. When the filling is cool, place one cup of filling on each layer. (Place first layer of cake topside down.)

CRANBERRY FILLING

2 1-lb. cans whole cranberry
    sauce
⅓ c. cornstarch
1 T. lemon juice
1 c. chopped blanched almonds

In a saucepan add cornstarch to cranberry sauce. Cook and stir over medium heat until thickened, boiling 2 minutes. Remove from heat and add lemon juice and almonds, stirring well. Cool. Frost entire cake with a fluffy frosting. Serves 12 to 18.

Lucille Pearces

APPLE-RAISIN RUM CAKE

½ c. butter
1 c. white sugar
½ c. brown sugar
2 eggs
2 c. flour
1½ t. baking powder
1 t. salt
½ t. baking soda
1 t. cinnamon
½ t. nutmeg
1 c. evaporated milk
2 T. rum
2 c. chopped apples
1 c. raisins
    Chopped nuts (optional)

In a bowl cream the butter, then beat in the sugars until light and fluffy. Beat in the eggs. Sift together the flour, baking powder, salt, soda, cinnamon and nutmeg. Add dry ingredients alternately with the undiluted evaporated milk and rum to the creamed mixture. Mix in the chopped apples, raisins and nuts.

Pour into a greased 9 x 12 x 2-inch baking pan. Bake in a 350° oven for about 40 minutes or until cake springs back when touched.

Helene Abric

HOLIDAY DATE CAKE

1 T. butter
1 c. sugar
1 egg
½ c. chopped nuts
1 t. vanilla
1 t. (level) baking soda
1 c. chopped dates
1 c. boiling water
1¼ c. all-purpose flour

Mix butter and sugar, then add egg, nuts and vanilla. Set aside. Sprinkle soda over dates, then pour boiling water over dates and soda. Cool. Add date mixture and flour to remaining ingredients and mix well. Bake in large loaf pan in a 350° oven 40 to 50 minutes.

Freda Murphy

WHITE FRUITCAKE
(Pictured)

1½ c. flour
    Pinch of salt
1 t. (level) baking powder
1 c. butter
1 c. sugar
4 eggs
1 c. candied fruit
1 T. flour
1 lemon, juice and grated rind

Combine 1½ cups flour, salt and baking powder. Into this rub the butter. Add sugar. Then add 2 of the eggs, unbeaten, and beat for 10 minutes. Add remaining eggs and beat another 10 minutes. Add candied fruit which has been cut in small pieces. Add the 1 tablespoon of flour and lemon rind and juice. Bake in a greased 9-inch springform for 1 hour at 350° or until done.

Note: This cake can also be baked in a well-greased and floured bundt cake pan.

Lorraine Obst

MINCEMEAT FRUITCAKE

1 jar (1-lb. 2-oz.) mincemeat (with rum and brandy)
1 c. broken pecans
1 c. white raisins
½ c. melted margarine
1 c. sugar
3 egg yolks
3 egg whites
1 t. baking soda
1 T. boiling water
2 c. sifted flour
1 t. vanilla

Put first 5 ingredients in a bowl. Add the egg yolks and baking soda dissolved in the boiling water. Then add flour. Fold in stiffly beaten egg whites and vanilla. Pour in a greased and floured bundt pan and bake at 300° for 1½ hours. Add 8 ounces candied fruit if desired.

Elizabeth Kizer

FRUIT CUPCAKES

1 c. walnuts, chopped
1½ c. mixed candied fruit
    and peels, chopped
1 14-oz. pkg. date bar mix
⅓ c. sifted flour
¾ t. baking powder
1 t. pumpkin pie spice
2 eggs, beaten
2 T. honey
½ c. thick applesauce
½ c. moist mincemeat
½ c. light raisins

Grease and flour cupcake pans. Turn contents of date bar mix into mixing bowl. Add flour, baking powder and spice, stirring to blend. Add eggs, honey, applesauce, mincemeat and raisins, beat well. Stir walnuts into fruit mixture. Spoon into prepared pans, filling about two-thirds full. Bake at 375° about 25 minutes or until toothpick inserted in center of cupcakes comes out clean. Makes 3 dozen.

Mrs. Jim Trulson

GUMDROP CAKE

1 c. shortening
2 c. sugar
2 eggs, beaten
1 lb. white raisins
2 lbs. colored gumdrops, chopped
    (do not use licorice-flavored
    gumdrops)
1½ c. cooked applesauce
½ t. salt
1 t. cinnamon
1 t. nutmeg
1 t. vanilla
1 t. orange extract
1 c. nutmeats, chopped
4 c. flour
1 T. water
1 t. baking soda

Sift together flour, salt, spices. Cream shortening. Add sugar and eggs. Beat well. Add applesauce, gumdrops which have been floured, nuts, raisins, flavorings, flour and soda dissolved in water. Put greased paper in bottom of pan. Bake 1 hour at 350°.

Minnie B. Mims

CHRISTMAS POUND CAKE

2 c. sugar
1 c. margarine
6 eggs
2 c. all-purpose flour
1 t. vanilla
4 t. lemon extract
8 ozs. candied pineapple
8 ozs. candied cherries
1 c. pecans, chopped
2 T. flour

Cream together thoroughly sugar and margarine. Add eggs. Add flour and flavorings and mix thoroughly. Add fruits and nuts that have been dredged in the 2 tablespoons flour. Bake at 325° in a lightly greased tube or bundt pan for 1 hour. Cool cake for 8 minutes after removing from oven, pour glaze over cake.

GLAZE

¼ c. margarine
1½ c. sugar
½ c. lemon juice
½ T. grated lemon rind

Heat all ingredients until sugar is dissolved. Pierce the surface of the cake with a fork while dribbling the glaze so glaze will soak into the cake. Cool before cutting.

Dot Curry

UPSIDE-DOWN PEAR GINGERBREAD CAKE

¼ c. (½ stick) butter
½ c. firmly packed light brown
    sugar
2 T. finely chopped maraschino
    cherries
2 c. thinly sliced fresh pears
    Orange or lemon juice
1 pkg. gingerbread mix
    Vanilla ice cream

In an 8-inch square baking pan melt butter; stir in sugar. Sprinkle cherries over butter and sugar. Dip pear slices in juice to prevent darkening. Arrange pear slices in rows over cherries. Set aside. Prepare gingerbread according to package directions. Pour over pears and bake according to package directions. Cool in pan on wire rack 5 minutes. Invert onto serving plate. Serve warm topped with vanilla ice cream.

TORTES

CRANBERRY TORTE

3 c. graham cracker crumbs
½ c. butter
2 c. sifted confectioners' sugar
1 egg
1 medium apple, ground
1 c. raw cranberries, ground
1 12-oz. can crushed pineapple, drained
1 c. granulated sugar
1 t. vanilla
1 pt. heavy cream, whipped

Pat graham cracker crumbs into a 12 x 7½-inch pan. Reserve ½ cup of the crumbs for topping. Cream butter, add confectioners' sugar gradually and continue creaming until fluffy. Add egg and mix well. Place over crumbs in pan. Then combine apple, cranberries, pineapple and sugar and spread over butter mixture. Add vanilla to whipped cream and spread over fruit mixture. Sprinkle reserved crumbs over top. Chill well. Makes 12 servings.

R. Hansen

EGGNOG TORTE

1 envelope unflavored gelatin
¼ c. cold water
¾ c. butter
1 c. confectioners' sugar
4 eggs, separated
⅓ c. dark rum or brandy
¾ c. chopped, toasted, salted almonds
¼ t. salt
1 c. heavy cream, whipped
1 10-inch angel food cake

Soften gelatin in the cold water about 5 minutes. Dissolve over hot water. Cream butter, gradually add sugar. Add egg yolks one at a time, beating well after each addition. Add rum and nuts and mix. Fold in slightly cooled gelatin. Add salt to egg whites and beat until stiff but not dry. Fold egg whites and whipped cream into first mixture. Pour over angel food cake that has been broken in small pieces. Blend lightly. Pour into an ungreased 10-inch springform pan. Refrigerate 2 to 3 hours. Serve with whipped cream and sprinkle with slivered almonds if desired.

J. Gaulke

EMPIRE TORTE

1 c. sifted all-purpose flour
1 t. double-acting baking powder
¾ c. sugar
4 egg whites
½ t. salt
½ t. cream of tartar
⅓ c. sugar
4 egg yolks
¼ c. water
1 t. vanilla
1 t. orange extract
Heavy-duty aluminum foil

Place an 18 x 12-inch sheet of heavy-duty aluminum foil on a baking sheet. Fold sides up to make a 16 x 10-inch pan. Make a second pan.

Sift flour with baking powder and ¾ cup sugar into a small mixing bowl. Beat egg whites, salt and cream of tartar in a large bowl until soft mounds form. Gradually add the ⅓ cup sugar, beating until stiff, straight peaks form. Do not underbeat.

Combine egg yolks, water and flavorings. Add to dry ingredients. Beat 1 minute at medium speed of electric mixer. Fold batter into beaten egg whites gently but thoroughly. Turn into the two foil pans. Spread batter evenly. Bake at 375° for 10 to 12 minutes. (Cakes may be baked one at a time.) Cool 10 minutes. Cut each cake into quarters. Remove foil. Cover tightly with aluminum foil until ready to frost.

Stack the 8 layers, spreading 2 to 3 tablespoons frosting between each layer. Frost sides and top. Garnish sides with chopped and whole walnuts. Chill at least 2 hours. Serves 10 to 12.

CHOCOLATE FROSTING

1 c. butter or margarine
2 squares (2 ozs.) cooled, melted unsweetened chocolate
1 t. vanilla
½ t. maple flavoring
2 c. sifted confectioners' sugar

Cream butter until fluffy. Add chocolate, flavorings and sugar. Blend, then beat at high speed of electric mixer until of spreading consistency.

Empire Torte

An easy, simple way of making thin-layered tortes has been found, using double-thick sheets of aluminum foil to form two long pans in which the batter can be thinly spread. The cake bakes very quickly in these foil pans and is soft and tender. The same delicate sponge cake baked in a jelly roll or layer cake pan is likely to dry out and get hard around the edges.

Each long cake was cut into squares to form the 8 layers needed. Then the layers were put together with a chocolate frosting and decorated with walnuts.

Since the torte needs to stand in the refrigerator for several hours before serving, a handsome chilling and serving tray may be made by covering a piece of heavy cardboard with aluminum foil.

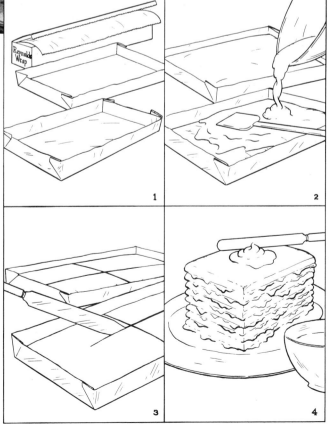

NESSELRODE PIE

3 eggs, separated
1 c. milk
¼ t. salt
⅔ c. sugar
1 T. unflavored gelatin
2 T. cold water
2 T. rum extract
¼ c. chopped maraschino cherries
½ c. heavy cream, whipped
1 8-inch baked piecrust

In the top of a double boiler, place the slightly beaten egg yolks, milk, salt and ½ cup of the sugar. Stir, then set over hot (not boiling) water until thick. Stir constantly, then remove. Soak gelatin in the water a few minutes, then stir into hot mixture until dissolved. Chill until syrupy.

Whip egg whites until stiff peaks form. Gradually add remaining sugar. Fold whipped cream into egg whites. Stir cherries and rum extract into gelatin mixture, then fold in whipped cream and egg whites. Pile into baked piecrust, garnish with grated sweet chocolate. Chill until firm.

GRASSHOPPER PIE

1⅓ c. honey graham crackers, crumbled
¼ c. sugar
¼ c. cocoa
¼ c. margarine, melted
¼ c. green creme de menthe
1 9-oz. jar marshmallow creme
2 c. heavy cream, whipped

Combine first 4 ingredients thoroughly. Press into a 9-inch pie pan. Reserve 2 tablespoons of mixture for topping. Bake at 375° for 8 minutes.

Gradually add creme de menthe to marshmallow creme. Beat until well blended. Fold whipped cream into marshmallow mixture. Pour into crust. Sprinkle with reserved crumbs around edge and center of pie. Freeze until firm. Serves 8.

Mrs. Richard Ford

EGGNOG WREATH PIE

1¼ c. graham cracker crumbs
¼ c. packed light brown sugar
⅓ c. melted butter or margarine
1 30-oz. can apricot halves, drained
1½ c. eggnog
2 eggs, separated
1 envelope unflavored gelatin
⅛ t. salt
Dash of nutmeg
2 T. brandy
¼ c. sugar
½ c. heavy or whipping cream, whipped
Red and green candied cherries

CRUST

Combine cracker crumbs, brown sugar and butter in a 9-inch pie plate and stir until crumbs are well coated. Press mixture into sides and bottom of pie plate. Bake in a 400° oven 8 minutes. Remove to wire rack to cool.

FILLING

Reserve 6 apricot halves for garnish. Into a blender place remaining drained apricots and puree until smooth. In top of a double boiler, add pureed apricots, the eggnog, egg yolks, gelatin, salt and nutmeg. Cook, stirring constantly, over hot (not boiling) water until gelatin dissolves and mixture coats spoon. Remove from heat, stir in brandy. Refrigerate apricot mixture in bowl until mixture mounds when dropped from a spoon. Meanwhile, beat egg whites until soft peaks form. Add sugar, 1 tablespoon at a time, and continue beating until stiff peaks form. Stir ¼ of this egg white mixture into cooked, cooled apricot mixture. Fold in remaining egg whites. Spoon into cooled crust. Refrigerate until set.

DECORATION

Arrange the 6 reserved, well-drained apricot halves upside-down on top of pie in circular "wreath-like" fashion. Make leaves for wreath by slicing cherries lengthwise into quarters. Place leaves next to apricot halves. Finish decoration by spooning or piping whipped cream into center of wreath. Garnish with a cluster of cherry pieces in center of whipped cream to resemble flower.

Photograph opposite
Eggnog Wreath Pie

SPECIAL CHOCOLATE PIE

    3 squares unsweetened chocolate
3½ c. milk
    1 egg or 2 egg yolks, slightly
      beaten
    ¾ c. sugar
    2 T. butter
    ⅔ c. sifted cake flour
1½ t. vanilla
    ¾ t. salt
    ½ c. cream, whipped
    1 c. chopped raisins or dates
    ¼ c. chopped nutmeats
    1 baked 9-inch piecrust

Add chocolate to milk and heat in a double boiler. When chocolate is melted, beat with a rotary egg beater until blended. Combine sugar, flour and salt. Add a small amount of chocolate mixture, stirring until smooth. Return to double boiler and cook until thick, stirring constantly. Then continue cooking 10 minutes, stirring occasionally.

Add a small amount of mixture to the egg, stirring vigorously. Return to double boiler and cook 2 more minutes, stirring constantly. Remove from boiling water. Add butter and vanilla. Cool slightly and turn into piecrust. Chill. Before serving cover with sweetened whipped cream to which raisins or dates have been added. Top with nutmeats.

Mrs. Paul E. King

SWEET POTATO PIE

1¼ c. cooked and mashed sweet
      potatoes
    3 eggs, beaten
    ½ c. brown sugar
    1 T. honey
    1 t. mace
    1 t. salt
    1 c. milk
    1 9-inch unbaked pie shell

Blend together above ingredients thoroughly. Pour into pie shell. Bake in a 425° oven 20 minutes. Then reduce heat to 350° and bake 25 to 30 minutes longer.

Marie M. Seymour

MINCEMEAT PIE

1½ c. flour
    1 t. salt
    ⅔ c. lard
    5 to 6 T. ice water

Sift flour and salt into a bowl. Mix in lard and blend with a pastry blender until mixture resembles fine cornmeal. Add ice water, tossing lightly until dough holds together in a ball, cleaning sides of bowl. Roll out on a floured pastry mat to a circle 1 inch larger than an inverted 9-inch pie pan. Fit loosely into the pan, trim off excess dough. Pour in the following filling. Add dots of butter and sprinkle with nutmeg. Add the top crust (make slits to let steam escape). Fold top edge under lower crust. Pinch edges to seal. Sprinkle top crust with sugar and drops of milk to make a brown glaze. Bake at 425° for 35 minutes.

FILLING

    2 c. mincemeat
    ½ c. orange marmalade
    2 T. flour
    1 T. lemon juice
    ¼ t. nutmeg

Combine all ingredients.

Mrs. B. G. Troutman

HOT WATER WHIPPED PIECRUST

    ¾ c. vegetable shortening
    ¼ c. boiling water
    1 T. milk
    2 c. flour
    1 t. salt

Put shortening in a mixing bowl. Add boiling water and milk. Tilt bowl and with rapid strokes beat until mixture is creamy and holds soft peaks. Sift flour and salt together. Add to mixture with round-the-bowl strokes until dough clings together and cleans bowl into smooth dough. Make a flat round and roll out between waxed paper. Makes two 9-inch flaky crusts.

Mrs. Fonda Crislip

CHRISTMAS PIE

1 3-oz. pkg. raspberry gelatin
1 c. boiling water
1 1-lb. can whole cranberry sauce
1 c. crushed pineapple, drained
2 c. miniature marshmallows
¼ c. sweet milk
½ t. vanilla
1 c. heavy cream, whipped
  Green food coloring
1 9-inch chilled graham cracker
  crust

Dissolve gelatin in boiling water. Chill until slightly thick. Fold in cranberry sauce and pineapple. Pour into graham cracker crust and chill until firm.

In a double boiler, melt marshmallows and milk. Stir until smooth. Add vanilla and a few drops of the green food coloring. Chill until thick. Mix until well blended. Fold in whipped cream. Spread over pie filling. Chill pie until firm.

Earna B. Banner

GRAHAM CRACKER CRUST

⅓ c. butter or margarine
2 T. sugar
1¼ c. graham cracker crumbs

Stir butter and sugar together in a saucepan over low heat until butter is melted. Blend in cracker crumbs. Press evenly into a 8- or 9-inch pie pan. Chill.

DIFFERENT PECAN PIE

3 egg whites, beaten
1 c. sugar
1 t. baking powder
1 c. graham cracker crumbs
1 c. chopped pecans

Beat egg whites until stiff. Beat in the sugar and baking powder. Stir in cracker crumbs and nuts. Pour into a greased pan and bake at 350° for 30 minutes. Serve topped with whipped cream if desired.

Myrtle M. Dubberly

HOLIDAY PIE

⅓ c. shortening
1 c. flour, sifted
2 T. cold water
¼ t. salt

Mix shortening in a bowl, add water and salt. Stir with a fork until thoroughly mixed. Add flour all at once, mixing lightly with a fork until well blended. Press into a ball and roll out to ⅛-inch thick. Fit loosely into a 9-inch pie pan. Flute edge. Cut some dough into the shape of a bell. Place on cookie sheet. Bake shell and cut-out bell in a 450° oven until golden brown.

FILLING

6 apples, peeled
½ c. raisins
½ c. nutmeats, chopped
1¼ c. sugar
1 c. cranberries
½ c. dates
3 T. flour
¾ c. water

Cut apples into thick slices. Combine with cranberries, raisins and dates. Sprinkle with flour. Bring sugar and water to a boil. Add fruit. Cook gently 10 minutes or until fruit is soft. Add a little more water if too dry to bubble gently. Cool slightly, add nuts. Cool. Arrange in baked piecrust. Decorate with bell cutout.

Margaret H. De Hass

FRUIT TURNOVERS

2 c. flour
1 c. margarine
1 c. small curd cottage cheese

Cream flour, margarine and cottage cheese. Chill for 4 hours. Drop by teaspoon on floured board and roll to 3-inch circles. Top with 1 teaspoon of fruit-flavored jam or canned fruit in center. Fold up sides, making a triangle. Pinch edges together at top. Bake at 425° until dough becomes "freckled." (Dough will freckle from the cottage cheese curds.) Serve warm.

Richard Ullman

PUDDINGS

CRANBERRY STEAMED PUDDING

1½ c. all-purpose flour
2 t. baking soda
2 c. fresh cranberries, halved
½ c. molasses
⅓ c. hot milk
½ c. chopped nuts

Into a bowl sift flour and baking soda. Stir in cranberries. Combine molasses and milk, stir into cranberry mixture until well blended. Stir in nuts. Turn into a 6-cup buttered mold. If mold has a lid, butter inside and cover (or press aluminum foil tightly around mold and secure with a string). Place mold on a rack in a pan with a tight cover. Pour about 1 inch of water into pan. Bring water to a boil and cover. Reduce heat to simmer. Steam for 2 hours. Remove mold to rack. Cool 10 minutes, then unmold.

SAUCE

½ c. butter
1 c. sugar
½ c. light cream
1 t. vanilla

In a 1-quart saucepan melt butter. Stir in sugar and cream until sugar dissolves. Bring to a boil, stirring occasionally. Stir in vanilla. Serve hot on pudding.

PRUNE PUDDING

1 lb. prunes
2½ c. water
⅔ c. cornstarch
½ c. water or prune juice
2 c. sugar
Juice of 1 lemon
1 c. nutmeats
1 t. cinnamon
Whipped cream

Cook prunes in the 2½ cups of water. Cool, pit and chop. Mix cornstarch in the ½ cup of water or prune juice. Add sugar, lemon juice, prunes and cornstarch mixture and cook slowly until thick and clear. Add nuts and cinnamon when lukewarm. Chill. Serve with whipped cream.

Leietta M. Taylor

CHRISTMAS PUDDING

¼ lb. suet, butter or margarine
½ c. brown sugar
1 large egg
1 c. grated raw carrots
½ c. seeded raisins
½ c. currants
1¼ c. flour
½ t. baking soda
1 t. baking powder
½ t. salt
1 T. warm water
½ t. cinnamon
½ t. nutmeg
(or ½ t. ground allspice)

With a large spoon, blend together first 3 ingredients. When well mixed add carrots, raisins and currants. Stir into the mixture the flour mixed with baking powder and salt. Put the 1 tablespoon warm water in a cup and add the ½ teaspoon baking soda. Stir into the flour and carrot mixture. Add spices and stir until all ingredients blend together. Place pudding into a greased mold, spreading it to corners. Seal. Stand up in enough water to reach just under the cover. Steam 1½ hours. Remove from water and cool. Bake 10 minutes at 350°. Remove from mold and place on a platter. Decorate with sprigs of holly and serve with the following hard sauce.

HARD SAUCE

½ c. butter or margarine
1 c. brown sugar
4 T. cream
½ t. lemon
Chopped nutmeats (optional)

Cream together butter and sugar. Add cream, lemon and nuts. Serve with Christmas Pudding.

Margaret Alves

Cranberry Steamed Pudding

DESSERTS

CREAM PUFF WREATH

1 c. water
1 c. sifted flour
½ c. butter
4 eggs

Place water and butter in a saucepan and bring to a boil. Gradually add flour to form a soft ball. Beat in eggs, one at a time. Continue beating until smooth. Drop on ungreased baking sheet according to size desired. Bake in a preheated 400° oven 45 minutes. Cool, cut off tops and fill with whipped cream, ice cream or a favorite filling. Arrange cream puffs around a bowl of chocolate sauce and drizzle sauce over puffs before serving.

Janice Fox

Candles in all shapes and colors will brighten a table or glow atop a mantel.

WINTER SNOWBALLS

1 box butter cookies
½ c. butter
1 c. sugar
2 eggs, separated
1 c. crushed pineapple,
    well drained
½ c. nutmeats
2 envelopes whipped topping
    Coconut

Cream butter, sugar and egg yolks thoroughly. Add pineapple and nuts. Beat egg whites until stiff and fold into mixture. Spread between individual butter cookies until 4 inches high. Chill overnight in refrigerator. Two or three hours before serving, cover with whipped topping and sprinkle with coconut. Tint coconut for added color if desired.

Margaret Seyfried

PLUM GOOD PARTY MOLD

2 cans (1-lb. 1-oz.) greengage plums
2 T. cornstarch
2 T. lemon juice
5 drops green food coloring
½ gal. vanilla ice cream,
    softened

Drain plums, reserve syrup. Pit plums, then sieve into a saucepan. Blend a few tablespoons syrup into cornstarch to make a smooth paste. Stir cornstarch mixture, remaining syrup, lemon juice and food coloring into plums. Cook, stirring constantly, until thick and clear. Chill. Pour ½ cup sauce into mold. Freeze. Set aside ¼ cup sauce for garnish. Fill mold, alternating layers of ice cream and sauce. Freeze. To serve, unmold and spoon reserved sauce over mold.

MARSHMALLOW SQUARES

¾ c. butter
⅓ c. brown sugar
1½ c. sifted all-purpose flour
2 T. unflavored gelatin
½ c. cold water
2 c. white sugar
½ c. hot water
½ c. drained, quartered maraschino
    cherries (or candied cherries)
¼ to ½ t. almond extract
    (or cherry juice)
2 drops red food coloring
½ c. chopped walnuts or almonds
    (optional)

Beat butter until creamy. Gradually add brown sugar, beating after each addition. Stir in flour. Press firmly into a 9 x 12-inch pan and bake at 325° until golden brown. Remove from oven and cool. Sprinkle gelatin over cold water and allow to soften. Combine white sugar and hot water in a saucepan. Place over high heat, stir and bring to a boil. Boil 2 minutes. Remove saucepan from heat and add softened gelatin. Beat with an electric mixer until very stiff. Fold in cherries, extract, coloring and nuts. Spoon over cooled shortbread layer. Cool. Cut in squares.

Esther Leaman

BOULE DE NEIGE

¼ c. rum, brandy or kirsch
1 c. mixed candied fruit
1 qt. vanilla ice cream
½ pt. heavy cream, whipped
2 T. sugar
1 t. vanilla
    Toasted flaked coconut

Add liquor to the candied fruit and let stand several hours, turning occasionally. Soften ice cream slightly. Line a 1½-quart bowl with aluminum foil, molding over the back, then fitting inside. Fold fruit into ice cream; quickly pack mixture into bowl. Cover with foil and place in freezer. To serve, loosen ice cream from bowl by tugging on foil. Unmold on cold plate. Remove foil. Whip cream, add sugar and vanilla. Frost ice cream with whipped cream. Top with toasted coconut. To serve, slice in wedges.

PEPPERMINT CANDY TORTE

1 chiffon cake
⅓ c. confectioners' sugar
1 c. crushed peppermint stick
  candy
2 drops red food coloring
1½ c. heavy cream, whipped
1 qt. strawberries

Cut cake into 2 layers. Fold sugar, candy and food coloring into cream. Put layers together with whipped cream mixture and cover top and sides. Garnish with strawberries.

PEPPERMINT FLUFF

2 T. finely crushed peppermint
  candy
1 pt. peppermint ice cream,
  softened
4 c. milk
1 c. whipping cream
  Peppermint ice cream
  Crushed peppermint candy

In a large mixing bowl, while beating the crushed candy and ice cream, gradually blend in milk and whipping cream. Beat until frothy. Pour into chilled glasses. Top each with a scoop of ice cream. Garnish with crushed candy.

PEPPERMINT ICE CREAM

1 c. milk
½ c. crushed peppermint stick
  candy
12 large marshmallows
¼ t. salt
1 c. heavy cream, whipped

Scald milk, add ¼ cup crushed candy, marshmallows and salt and stir until dissolved. Freeze in refrigerator tray until firm, about 2 hours. Beat in a chilled bowl until smooth. Fold in remaining candy and whipped cream and return to tray to freeze until firm, about 3 to 4 hours.

Charlotte Russe

CATHEDRAL WINDOW COOKIES

1 12-oz. pkg. chocolate chips
½ c. butter or margarine
½ c. ground nuts (optional)
1 10½-oz. pkg. colored miniature
   marshmallows
2 eggs, well beaten
   Confectioners' sugar

Slowly melt the butter and chocolate chips. Remove from heat and add eggs and nuts. Cool. Add marshmallows in 2 or 3 additions. Mix well. Sprinkle confectioners' sugar on three pieces of waxed paper. Divide mixture into three rolls, using more confectioners' sugar on hands and top. Chill a few hours or overnight. Slice and serve.

Mrs. D. L. Manker

SUGAR COOKIES

4 c. sifted cake flour
2½ t. baking powder
½ t. salt
⅔ c. shortening
1½ c. sugar
2 eggs, unbeaten
1 t. vanilla
4 t. milk

Sift flour, baking powder, salt. Mix shortening with sugar, eggs and vanilla until very light and fluffy. Mix flour mixture alternately with milk. Refrigerate dough until easy to handle. On a floured surface, roll a half or a third of dough at a time, keeping rest in refrigerator. For crisp cookies roll dough thin. Cut into desired shapes. Arrange cookies on a greased cookie sheet ½ inch apart. Decorate with white or colored sugar, chopped nuts, flaked coconut, cinnamon or candied fruit. Bake 9 minutes in a 400° oven. Makes about 6 dozen. (Clean strings can be pressed into the cookies to form a loop so they can be hung on the Christmas tree.)

Photograph opposite:
Sugar Cookies
Glazed Lebkuchen, p. 48
Springerle, p. 48
Gingerbread Cookies, p. 49

CHRISTMAS SEED COOKIES

2½ c. sifted cake flour
½ t. baking powder
⅛ t. salt
1 c. sugar
1 c. soft butter
2 egg yolks
1 t. vanilla
   Seed such as caraway, sesame,
   poppy

Sift the dry ingredients, cut in butter. Add egg yolks and vanilla. Blend. Chill the mixture several hours, then roll to ⅛-inch thickness and cut in fancy shapes. Place on cookie sheets and sprinkle with seed. Bake in a 400° oven for about 8 minutes. Makes 8 dozen.

RAISIN-CURRANT BARS

1½ c. sifted all-purpose flour
1 t. baking powder
1 c. firmly packed brown sugar
1½ c. quick-cooking rolled oats
¾ c. butter

Combine all ingredients, making a crumbly mixture. Pat two-thirds of the mixture into a greased 13 x 9 x 2-inch baking pan. Spread with the following filling. Cover with remaining crumbs. Bake at 350° for 35 minutes. Cool and cut into bars. Makes 3½ dozen.

FRUIT-SPICE FILLING

1 c. raisins
1 c. currants
1½ c. hot water
1 c. sugar
2 T. all-purpose flour
1 t. cinnamon
½ t. cloves
1 t. vinegar
1 T. butter

Combine all ingredients in a saucepan. Bring to a boil and continue cooking until thick, stirring occasionally.

Mrs. Richard DeLong

SPRINGERLE

2 eggs
1 c. sugar
2 c. sifted all-purpose flour
¼ t. salt
1 t. baking powder
1 t. anise extract or anise seed

Beat eggs at high speed in small bowl of electric mixer until thick and light colored. Add sugar very gradually. Turn mixer to low speed; beat until sugar is dissolved. (This takes about 10 minutes.) Fold in sifted dry ingredients and anise. Place a small portion of dough at a time on well-floured canvas; coat dough with flour; pat with palms of hands to ⅓-inch thickness. Dust springerle rolling pin with flour; press on dough to emboss the designs and get a clear imprint. Work quickly. Cut out the squares; place on greased cookie sheets; allow to dry at room temperature 4 to 6 hours. Bake at 350° for 10 to 12 minutes. Cool. Store in a covered container to mellow and soften. Makes about 3 dozen.

GLAZED LEBKUCHEN

¾ c. honey
½ c. granulated sugar
¼ c. brown sugar, packed
2 eggs, beaten
2½ c. sifted all-purpose flour
1 t. baking soda
¼ t. cloves
1¼ t. cinnamon
⅛ t. allspice
½ c. finely chopped citron
½ c. finely chopped candied lemon
   peel
¾ c. chopped blanched almonds
1 c. confectioners' sugar
3 T. hot milk
¼ t. vanilla
   Candied cherries, citron

Bring honey to a boil; cool. Add sugars and eggs, beat well. Blend in sifted dry ingredients, fruit and almonds. Spread into a greased 10 x 15 x 1-inch pan. Bake at 350° about 25 minutes. Blend confectioners' sugar, milk and vanilla; spread over top. Decorate with fruits. Cut into bars. Makes 2 dozen.

Springerle

CHRISTMAS CANDLE COOKIES

2 c. sugar
1 c. margarine
2 eggs
1 c. milk
7 c. flour
6 t. baking powder
1 t. salt
2 t. vanilla

Mix above ingredients together. Roll to ½ inch, cut with cookie cutter or make desired pattern with cardboard. (A 1 x 4-inch piece of cardboard with the top inch fashioned into flame shape makes the candle pattern.) Place cut cookies on lightly greased tins. Bake 7 to 10 minutes in a 390° oven until edges are lightly browned. Frost with the following icing:

ICING

2 T. shortening
2 T. light corn syrup
Flavoring to taste
Milk
Confectioners' sugar

Combine shortening, syrup and flavoring. Add enough milk and sugar for desired consistency.

This recipe can also be used to make jam tarts by cutting rounds, placing a teaspoonful of jam on one round, covering with another and sealing the edges. Increase baking time by 2 to 3 minutes.

Pollyanna Sedziol

CINNAMON KRINKLES

2⅔ c. sifted flour
2 t. cream of tartar
2 t. baking soda
½ t. salt
1 c. butter
1½ c. sugar
2 eggs

Sift together flour, cream of tartar, baking soda and salt. Cream butter and sugar. Add eggs one at a time. Beat well. Add dry ingredients. Refrigerate for 1 hour. Place on greased pans in a 350° oven 12 to 15 minutes. Combine 2 tablespoons cinnamon and 3 tablespoons sugar. Roll on cookie dough.

Carol Knudson

GINGERBREAD COOKIES

2 c. flour
1 t. baking powder
¼ t. baking soda
1 t. cinnamon
½ t. ginger
⅓ c. sugar
½ c. shortening
½ c. molasses
3 T. hot water

Combine all ingredients in a large bowl. Blend well. Chill dough at least 1 hour before handling. Roll out dough on floured surface to ⅛-inch thickness. Use gingerbread man cookie cutter. Place on ungreased cookie sheets. Bake at 400° for 8 to 10 minutes. Cool and decorate.

ALMOND CRESCENTS

1 c. soft butter or margarine
½ c. plus 1 T. confectioners' sugar
1 egg yolk
1 t. vanilla
1 t. almond extract
2 c. sifted flour
1 c. finely chopped nuts
Confectioners' sugar

Cream butter and sugar and beat well. Add egg yolk and flavorings and beat to blend. Add flour gradually, mixing until moistened. Add nuts and blend. Form into small crescents about 2½ inches long and bake on an ungreased cookie sheet in a 350° oven 20 minutes or until slightly golden. Remove from oven. Sprinkle with confectioners' sugar. Makes 40.

Stanley R. Rempala

FILLED COOKIES

4 c. brown sugar
¾ c. butter or margarine
4 eggs
1 t. cream of tartar
1 t. baking soda
6 c. flour
1 t. vanilla

Blend sugar and butter. Add eggs one at a time. Sift together cream of tartar, baking soda and flour and add to sugar and butter. Beat well. Add vanilla. Roll out on a floured surface and cut into circles. Place about a tablespoon of the following filling in the center of one circle. Place a second circle on top of filling. Press together. Bake at 350° for 8 to 10 minutes on a greased cookie sheet.

FILLING

2½ c. raisins
2 T. cornstarch
2 T. water
1 c. sugar
1 c. nuts

Place raisins in a saucepan and add enough water to cover. Cook over low heat until tender. Make a paste of the cornstarch and 2 tablespoons of water. Add this paste and the sugar to raisins. Mix well. Add nuts.

Mrs. Archie Ridall

CHOCOLATE NUT PUFFS

1 c. (6 ozs.) semisweet chocolate pieces
2 egg whites
½ c. sugar
½ t. vinegar
¾ c. chopped nuts
⅛ t. salt
½ t. vanilla

Preheat oven to 350°. Grease cookie sheet. Melt chocolate over warm water. Beat egg whites with salt until foamy. Gradually add sugar. Beat until stiff peaks form. Beat in vanilla and vinegar. Fold in melted chocolate and nuts. Drop by teaspoonful on cookie sheet. Bake about 10 minutes. Makes 3 dozen.

Rosalie L. Kennedy

CHRISTMAS DROP COOKIES

1 lb. dates
½ lb. blanched almonds
½ lb. walnuts
½ lb. Brazil nuts
3 slices candied pineapple
(red, yellow and green)
½ c. flour
½ c. butter
1 c. flour
¼ t. salt
¾ c. brown sugar
1 large egg, beaten
½ t. baking soda
½ t. vanilla

Cut up dates, nuts and candied pineapple slices. Add ½ cup flour to nuts and fruit, mixing thoroughly. Cream butter and sugar. Add beaten egg and vanilla to creamed mixture. Then mix in 1 cup flour, soda and salt. Add floured nuts and fruit. Mix well. Drop by teaspoon on a greased cookie sheet and bake 15 minutes in a 350° oven. After cooling, place cookies in containers with a tight lid and store a week before using. Makes about 8 dozen.

Mrs. A. M. Anderson

PECAN BALLS

1 c. margarine
¼ c. sugar
2 c. sifted flour
2 c. pecans, broken into
small pieces
Confectioners' sugar
Granulated sugar

Cream margarine, sugar and flour. Add pecans and mix well. Use 1 tablespoon of dough for each cookie and shape into balls. Bake in a 300° oven on an ungreased cookie sheet about 45 minutes. Roll in mixed confectioners' and granulated sugar as soon as removed from oven. Makes about 4 dozen.

Mary Robinson

CANDIES

MARZIPAN

¼ c. margarine
¼ c. light corn syrup
¼ t. salt
½ t. lemon or vanilla extract
1 lb. confectioners' sugar
1 c. almond paste
Food coloring

Cream margarine, then blend in syrup, salt and flavoring. Add sugar a third at a time and mix well after each addition. Knead in almond paste. Color with a few drops of food coloring. Mold into small shapes of fruits and vegetables or use as the center for candied cherries, dates and prunes.

For tree trims, use little marzipan fruits...cookies of many shapes and sizes, strung together or hung like ornaments on their own thread loops.

CHRISTMAS PUDDING CANDY

3 c. sugar
1 c. light cream
1 T. (heaping) butter
1 t. vanilla
1 lb. dates
1 lb. figs
1 lb. raisins
1 lb. coconut
1 or 2 c. nuts

Cook sugar, cream and butter to soft-ball stage (about 236° on a candy thermometer). Add vanilla. Beat until creamy, then beat in fruit and nuts. Grind coconut if coarse. When well mixed, roll in a loaf. Wrap in dampened cloth, then in waxed paper, and store in a cool place at least 2 weeks. Slice in squares, rounds and oblongs when ready to serve.

Golde Hoover

FAIRY FOOD

1 c. sugar
1 c. light corn syrup
1 T. vinegar
1½ T. baking soda
1 6-oz. pkg. semisweet chocolate bits, melted

Mix sugar, syrup and vinegar in a 3-quart saucepan. Cook to hard-crack stage (300° on a candy thermometer). Remove from heat. Add baking soda and mix quickly. Pour into a greased 11 x 7 x 1½-inch pan. Cool. Invert on a tray and spread with melted chocolate. Break into chunks. Makes 1 pound.

Mrs. Peter Tyndale

HOLIDAY PRALINES

1 c. brown sugar
1 c. white sugar
1 c. thin cream
⅛ t. salt
3 T. butter
1 c. chopped pecans
1 T. maple syrup

Bring first 3 ingredients to a boil and boil hard for 1 minutes. Add remaining ingredients and cook to soft-ball stage (234° on a candy thermometer). Stir at once and drop by teaspoonsful on waxed paper.

Lorene Kuepfer

BUTTER TOFFEE

2¼ c. sugar
1 t. salt
½ c. water
1¼ c. butter
1½ c. (½ lb.) chopped blanched almonds
1 c. finely chopped walnuts
¼ lb. milk chocolate, melted

Bring sugar, salt, water and butter to a boil. Add half of the almonds. Cook, stirring constantly, to the hard-crack stage (290° on a candy thermometer). Remove from heat. Add remaining almonds and half of the walnuts. Pour into a greased, shallow 9 x 13-inch pan. Cool. Brush with melted chocolate and sprinkle with remaining walnuts. Break into pieces.

TINY TIM ORANGES

Using the point of a paring knife, remove peel in quarters from 4 medium oranges. Cover peel with cold water and simmer in a saucepan until tender. Drain well. Reserve 1 cup of the water in which peel was cooked. Put orange peel through a food chopper, using coarse blades. Combine 2 cups sugar and 1 cup reserved orange liquid. Stir over low heat until sugar dissolves. Cook to 238° on a candy thermometer, or until a little of the mixture forms a soft ball when dropped in cold water.

Add orange peel, simmer 10 minutes or until most of the liquid has evaporated. Spread in buttered shallow pan. When cool enough to handle, form into balls about ¾-inch in diameter. Roll in granulated sugar to which a small amount of orange food coloring has been added. Makes 40 oranges.

Mrs. Charles P. Kinery

MAPLE BUTTERNUT CANDY

6 c. white sugar
4 c. maple syrup
¼ c. butter

Cook to form a soft ball when dropped into cold water. Remove from heat. Stir in 2 c. chopped or ground butternut meats. Stir until thick enough so that butternuts do not rise to the top. Pour into two 13 x 8-inch greased pans.

Mrs. Van B. Slack

FROSTIES

Cook 8 marshmallows and ¼ cup evaporated milk in top of a double boiler, stirring constantly. When marshmallows dissolve remove from heat but leave mixture over hot water. Cut 12 marshmallows in half. Dip marshmallows one at a time into mixture. Drop on waxed paper after rolling in 1½ cups shredded coconut. The coconut may be toasted a light brown if desired.

Golde Hoover

CANDY STRAWBERRIES

2 large pkgs. wild strawberry gelatin
1 can sweetened condensed milk
1 lb. shredded coconut
1 t. almond extract

Put coconut through blender. Mix all ingredients together. Shape into strawberries. Roll in red crystal sugar. Insert strawberry stems.

Note: If stems are unavailable, roll top part of strawberry in green crystal sugar.

Mrs. R. C. Sauer

HARD CANDY

1¾ c. sugar
½ c. light corn syrup
½ c. water
1 t. flavoring
Food coloring

Combine sugar, corn syrup and water in a saucepan. Bring to a boil over medium heat until mixture reaches 300° on a candy thermometer. Remove from heat and add flavoring and a few drops of food coloring. For variety, divide mixture in half and add ½ teaspoon each of different flavorings and colors. Pour onto marble slab to cool. Then cut with scissors or break with knife into strips. Store in glass jars.

LEMON TAFFY

1½ c. sugar
¾ c. water
½ t. cream of tartar
⅓ t. lemon extract

Boil above ingredients without stirring until brittle when dropped in cold water (300° on a candy thermometer). Cool slightly. Butter hands. Pull with tips of fingers and thumbs until taffy is light and creamy. Set aside to harden. Then break into chunks. Store in airtight containers.

Donna Kingsley

NO-COOK CHOCOLATE FUDGE

1 lb. confectioners' sugar
2 eggs, well beaten
1 c. broken nutmeats
1 t. vanilla
6 sqs. unsweetened chocolate
2 T. butter

Sift sugar and gradually add to the eggs. Mix until smooth. Add nuts and vanilla. Melt chocolate slowly in the top of a double boiler. Stir constantly while melting. Add butter to melted chocolate and blend. Add chocolate mixture to nut mixture and mix well. Turn at once into a 10 x 6-inch well-greased pan. When firm, cut into pieces. Yields about 2 pounds.

Diane M. Marple

CHRISTMAS PEANUT BRITTLE

When it is Christmas candy time,
Or any time of year,
This peanut brittle recipe
Becomes especially dear.
You add to one large cooking pan
A cup of each of these —
White syrup, sugar, water too
And blend with gentle ease.

A teaspoonful of table salt,
When it is added too,
Will mean that you have reached the point
When you must cook the brew.
So cook it to the soft ball stage
And then it's time to add
A tablespoon of butter
And the peanuts to your pan.

It takes one pound of peanuts
That you've purchased in the shell,
And shucked yourself ahead of time
To make this turn out well.
With all ingredients in the pan
You cook until it's brown,
And take your pan from off the stove —
Your candy's almost done.

Stir in one teaspoon soda,
Pour on a buttered sheet,
And let it harden as it will,
Then break in chunks your treat.
The rest comes very naturally
Just eat to suit your will,
And have a happy holiday
That's peanut brittle filled.

Craig E. Sathoff

RAINBOW POPCORN BALLS

6 T. salad oil
1 c. light corn syrup
½ c. sugar
1 3-oz. pkg. strawberry or lime gelatin
1½ c. salted peanuts, coarsely chopped
½ c. sugar
½ c. unpopped corn
Red or green food coloring

To pop corn, heat 6 tablespoons oil over medium heat. Add ½ cup popcorn in a single layer. Heat until all corn is popped. Turn into a bowl, add peanuts to popcorn and toss to mix.

In a 1-quart saucepan combine corn syrup and sugar. Cook, stirring with a wooden spoon, until sugar dissolves. Without stirring, bring mixture to a full rolling boil. Remove from heat and add gelatin. Stir until dissolved and add food coloring. Pour over popcorn and mix. Butter hands and form into balls.

Julia K. Chapman

MAPLE SEAFOAM

3 c. light brown sugar, firmly packed
¾ c. water
1 T. maple syrup
2 egg whites
⅛ t. salt
1 t. vanilla
1 t. maple flavoring
1½ c. broken walnuts (optional)

Mix sugar, water and maple syrup. Stir over low heat until the boiling point is reached. Boil quickly to 238° on a candy thermometer or until a few drops form a soft ball when dropped in cold water.

Beat egg whites with the salt until stiff. Pour sugar syrup over egg whites in a thin stream, beating constantly. Continue beating until thick and creamy. Add flavorings and nuts. Drop from a teaspoon onto a well-greased pan.

Photograph opposite Seafoam, fudge, peanut brittle and popcorn balls.

ORANGE EGGNOG PUNCH

1 pt. pineapple juice
2 c. chilled orange juice
1 qt. dairy eggnog
Raspberry, orange or lime sherbet

In a mixing bowl, beat sherbet until smooth. Add juices and blend thoroughly. Gradually add eggnog. Pour into punch bowl. Float small scoops of sherbet on top.

NEW YEAR'S HERRING DIP

1 8-oz. pkg. cream cheese, softened
2 T. chopped pimiento
1 8-oz. jar herring fillets in wine sauce, drained
1 c. cottage cheese

Combine cream cheese and pimiento. Cut herring in small pieces. Fold herring and cottage cheese into cream cheese. Heat mixture over low heat until hot and bubbly. Transfer to a chafing dish and keep warm. Add herring liquid as needed for dipping consistency. Serve with assorted crackers.

Julia P. Oscar

PICKLED SHRIMP

½ clove garlic
1 t. salt
½ c. cider vinegar
¼ c. salad oil
4 drops tabasco
2 T. chopped stuffed olives
3 T. minced parsley
2 T. chopped dill pickle
2 lbs. cooked and cleaned jumbo shrimp

Mash garlic and salt together. Add all ingredients and place in a quart jar. Shake well. Place in refrigerator at least 24 hours before serving. Serve with slivers of pumpernickel bread. Yield: 12 servings.

Carrie Nelson

HAM AND CHEESE SPECIALS

2 8-oz. cans sliced pineapple in unsweetened pineapple juice
2 3-oz. pkgs. cream cheese, softened
2 t. ground cinnamon
1 16-oz. can brown bread, cut in 8 slices
8 slices boiled ham
1 10½-oz. can chicken gravy

Drain pineapple, reserving 5 tablespoons of juice. Combine cream cheese and cinnamon. Spread about 1 tablespoon on each slice of bread. Top with ham and pineapple. Broil 4 inches from heat 5 minutes or until hot.

In a saucepan blend gravy and reserved pineapple juice into remaining cream cheese mixture. Heat, stirring occasionally. Serve over sandwiches. Makes 8 open-face sandwiches.

SAUSAGE AND OYSTER CASSEROLE

3 c. elbow macaroni, cooked
1 lb. pork sausage, cut into
   1-inch pieces
½ c. onions, chopped
2 cans cream of celery soup
1½ t. salt
¼ t. pepper
1 small can button mushrooms
1 c. milk
½ c. chopped parsley
1 pt. oysters

Fry sausage slowly in a skillet until lightly browned. Remove sausage to paper towels. Pour off half of the fat. Add mushrooms and onion to remaining fat and sauté until onion is transparent. Stir in soup, milk, seasoning and parsley. Cook until thoroughly heated. Add oysters and half of the browned sausage. Mix. Heat thoroughly. In a greased 3-quart casserole, alternately layer macaroni and sausage-oyster mixture. Top with remaining sausage. Bake at 350° for ½ hour.

Mrs. Frank Watembach

SNOWBALL CAKE

2½ pkgs. unflavored gelatin
2½ c. sliced pineapple, drained
1 c. sugar
5 pkgs. whipped topping
   (2 to pkg.)
1 angel food cake
1 c. pecans, chopped
1 can flaked coconut
½ t. vanilla
1 T. lemon juice

Dissolve gelatin in 5 tablespoons water. Add 1 cup boiling water. Add pineapple, sugar and lemon juice to gelatin and mix. Place in refrigerator until thick.

Whip 4 packages whipped topping. Break cake into bite-size pieces. Add cake to the whipped topping. Then add nuts and vanilla. Add to mixture in refrigerator. Put in buttered tube pan. Let set overnight. Whip remaining whipped topping and ice cake. Sprinkle with flaked coconut.

Mrs. G. A. Hoffman

Ham and Cheese Specials

LEMON CHAMPAGNE SPARKLER

4 6-oz. cans frozen concentrated
   lemonade
4 6-oz. cans frozen pineapple juice
1½ qts. water
2 qts. ginger ale, chilled
1 qt. sparkling water, chilled
1 bottle (⅘ qt.) dry champagne,
   chilled

Mix concentrated lemonade, pineapple juice and water. Chill, covered. Before serving add ginger ale and sparkling water and pour in a large punch bowl. Add ice cubes. Pour champagne over punch and stir.

Mrs. R. W. Norton

COCONUT CHRISTMAS COOKIE TREE

1½ c. butter or margarine
1 c. sugar
2 eggs
4½ c. sifted all-purpose flour
1 t. vanilla
1 t. almond extract
4 T. hot milk
1 lb. unsifted confectioners' sugar
Flaked coconut

Cut star-shaped patterns from heavy paper 9, 8, 7¼, 6½, 5½, 4¾, 4, and 3 inches in diameter, measuring from point to point. Cut two round patterns 2½ and 1½ inches in diameter.

Cream butter until soft. Gradually add sugar, beating until light and fluffy. Add eggs and beat well. Add flour, a small amount at a time, mixing thoroughly after each addition. Blend in vanilla, almond extract and 2 cups of the coconut (cut). Divide dough into 2 equal portions, wrap in waxed paper and chill at least 30 minutes or until firm enough to roll.

Roll dough ⅛-inch thick on a lightly floured board. Cut 2 cookies from each star pattern, making a total of 16 cookies. Cut 12 cookies from the 1½-inch round pattern and 20 cookies from the 2½-inch round pattern. With a large drinking straw, cut a hole in the center of each cookie. Place on ungreased baking sheets. Bake at 350° for about 8 minutes, or until edges are lightly browned. Cool.

Gradually add hot milk to the confectioners' sugar, using just enough milk for a spreading consistency. Tint green with food coloring if desired. Spread on each star-shaped cookie. Sprinkle flaked coconut near edges.

TO MAKE TREE

Place a 12- to 15-inch stick or thin candle in a candle holder. Secure with short stub of a candle or with paper. Slip 2 of the larger round cookies over stick. Top with largest star cookie and decrease to smallest size, placing 2 round cookies between each star-shaped cookie. Top with a rosette of frosting or a small candle. Decorate with silver dragées or small candles if desired. Makes 1 cookie tree.

GIFTS FROM THE KITCHEN

STRIPED COOKIES

2½ c. sifted cake flour
1 t. double-acting baking powder
½ t. salt
½ c. butter or margarine
⅔ c. sugar
1 egg
1 T. milk
1 square unsweetened chocolate, melted
Milk

Sift flour with baking powder and salt. Cream butter. Gradually add sugar. Beat until light and fluffy. Add egg and milk. Blend well. Add flour mixture, a small amount at a time, beating well after each addition. Divide dough in half. Blend chocolate into one half. If necessary chill or freeze both parts of dough until firm enough to roll.

Roll each portion of dough on a lightly floured board into a 9 x 4½-inch rectangle. Brush chocolate dough lightly with milk and top with plain dough. Using a long, sharp knife, cut rectangle lengthwise in 3 equal strips 1½ inches wide.

Stack strips, alternating colors, brushing each layer with milk and pressing together lightly. Carefully wrap in waxed paper. Freeze until firm enough to slice, or chill overnight in refrigerator.

Cut in ⅛-inch slices, using a very sharp knife. Place on greased baking sheets. Bake at 400° for 6 to 8 minutes or just until white portions begin to brown. Makes about 5½ dozen.

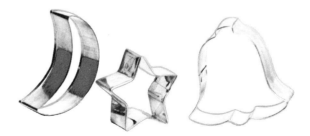

It's nice at Christmastime to give gifts of food from your kitchen. A fragrant applesauce or nut cake...fruitcake, cookies that are easy to make, a holiday pie. The list of foods appropriate for gift-giving is long.

Most can be prepared a few days before Christmas. Aluminum foil can help with the preparation and can also be used for wrapping.

A handsome aluminum mold or pan filled with a holiday cake, pie or bread will make a long-remembered gift. Stores are filled with rings and molds of many shapes. Some are natural silver in color while others are gay copper-toned aluminum.

Aluminum pans are wonderful bakers that withstand oven temperatures. If you bake ahead and freeze, cover the food with an air-tight lid of foil, sealed to the edges, and foods will keep for months.

Leave foil in place during the 1 or 2 hours at room temperature that it takes to thaw the foods. Then add gift wrapping of foil and the food will remain fresh for several days.

SPICY APPLESAUCE CAKE

- 2 c. sifted all-purpose flour
- 1½ t. baking soda
- ½ t. salt
- ½ t. each: cinnamon, ground cloves, nutmeg, allspice
- ½ c. butter or margarine
- 1 t. vanilla
- 1 c. light brown sugar, firmly packed
- ½ c. white sugar
- 2 eggs, lightly beaten
- 1½ c. sweetened applesauce
- ¾ c. each: dates, raisins, broken walnuts
  Confectioners' sugar

Line an ungreased 9 x 5 x 3-inch loaf pan with aluminum foil. Sift flour with soda, salt and spices. Cream butter with vanilla and sugars until light and fluffy. Add eggs and continue beating until very light. Add flour mixture alternately with the applesauce, stirring until just blended. Cut dates in small pieces and combine with the raisins and walnuts. Fold in lightly. Turn into foil-lined loaf pan, saving a few spoonsful to bake in a small foil pan for testing. Bake 1 hour at 325° or until cake is firm and springy when touched. Cool and sprinkle with confectioners' sugar before wrapping in foil.

A gift,
however small,
speaks its
own language.

Norman Vincent Peale

STUFFED DATES

Purchase pitted dates or ones with pits and remove pits. Fill centers with one or more of the following: walnut or pecan meats, peanut butter mixed with chopped peanuts, plain fondant or fondant mixed with chopped candied fruits. Roll in confectioners' sugar or finely grated coconut. Keeps well in an airtight container in the refrigerator.

CANDIED ORANGE COFFEE CAKE

- ¾ c. sugar
- ¼ c. butter or margarine
- 1 egg
- ½ c. milk
- 1½ c. sifted all-purpose flour
- 2 t. double-acting baking powder
- ½ t. salt
- 4 t. candied orange peel, finely minced
- 1 T. grated orange rind

Blend sugar, butter and egg until light and fluffy. Add milk and dry ingredients alternately, then orange peel and rind, stirring until just combined. Pour into a greased star-shape mold (9 inches from point to point). Sprinkle with the following topping. Bake in a 375° oven for 25 to 30 minutes. To freeze, cool and then cover top of pan with aluminum foil. Seal to edge by crimping. To serve, remove foil and heat in a 350° oven 20 minutes if frozen and 10 minutes if defrosted.

TOPPING

- ½ c. sugar
- ⅓ c. all-purpose flour
- 1 T. grated orange rind
- 4 T. candied orange peel, chopped
- ¼ c. butter or margarine

Blend all ingredients together to crumb consistency.

MOCK FONDANT BALLS

- ½ c. butter
- 1 lb. confectioners' sugar
- ¼ c. heavy cream
- 1 t. vanilla
  Hazelnuts, pecans or walnuts
  Candied fruit, cut in small pieces

With an electric mixer, cream butter until light, add sugar gradually. When very thick start adding cream and vanilla a little at a time. Mixture will become too heavy for the electric mixer, so remove beaters and turn out on a board sprinkled with remaining sugar. With hands, knead in remaining sugar. Break off small pieces of the mixture (about 2 teaspoons) and form around a nutmeat or pieces of candied pineapple or small pieces of candied orange peel. Form into balls and roll in confectioners' sugar. Store in airtight container in refrigerator.